WILLIAM SHAKESPEARE'S
LONG LOST FIRST PLAY
(abridged)

WILLIAM SHAKESPEARE'S
LONG LOST FIRST PLAY
(abridged)

by Reed Martin and Austin Tichenor

JOSEF WEINBERGER PLAYS

LONDON

WILLIAM SHAKESPEARE'S LONG LOST FIRST PLAY (ABRIDGED)
First published in 2018
by Josef Weinberger Ltd
12-14 Mortimer Street, London W1T 3JJ
www.josef-weinberger.com / plays@jwmail.co.uk

ISBN: 978 0 85676 372 4

IMPORTANT NOTE:

The name "Reduced Shakespeare Company" ® is a Registered Trademark, and its use in any way whatsoever to publicise, promote, or advertise any performance of this script is EXPRESSLY PROHIBITED.

Likewise, any use of the name "Reduced Shakespeare Company" ® within the actual live performance of this script is also EXPRESSLY PROHIBITED.

The play must be billed as follows:

WILLIAM SHAKESPEARE'S LONG LOST FIRST PLAY
(abridged)

By
REED MARTIN & AUSTIN TICHENOR

Folger Shakespeare Library Editions are the Official Complete Works Resource for this play.

ABOUT THE AUTHORS

Reed Martin

Reed co-created and performed in the original RSC productions of *America, Bible, Western Civilization, All The Great Books, Hollywood, Sports, Christmas*, and *Comedy — all (abridged)*. He also contributed additional material to *The Complete Works of William Shakespeare (abridged)*, and is the co-author of *Pop-Up Shakespeare* (illustrated by Jennie Maizels). He has performed in London's West End, at Lincoln Center, Kennedy Center, Seattle Repertory Theatre, American Repertory Theatre, Pittsburgh Public Theater, ACT San Francisco, McCarter Theatre, Old Globe Theatre, La Jolla Playhouse, The White House and Madison Square Garden, as well as in 11 foreign countries. He toured for two years as a clown/assistant ringmaster with Ringling Brothers/Barnum & Bailey Circus. Reed has written for the BBC, National Public Radio, TBS, Britain's Channel Four, RTE Ireland, Public Radio International, Sky TV UK, the Washington Post, and Vogue magazine. Reed's work has been nominated for an Olivier Award in London, a Helen Hayes Award in Washington, DC, and a San Francisco Bay Area Theater Critic's Circle Award. He lives in Northern California with his wife and two sons, all three of whom are much funnier than he is.

Austin Tichenor

Austin has performed with the RSC around the world, off-Broadway, in London's West End, and in the PBS version of *The Complete Works of William Shakespeare (abridged)*. He has written stage adaptations of *Frankenstein*, a Kafka-for-kids adaptation of "The Metamorphosis" called *Dancing on the Ceiling*, and (with Reed Martin) P*op-Up Shakespeare* (illustrated by Jennie Maizels), the irreverent reference book *Reduced Shakespeare: The Complete Guide for the Attention-Impaired (abridged)*, the comic e-book memoir *How The Bible Changed Our Lives (Mostly For The Better)*, and the stage comedies *America, Bible, Western Civilization, All The Great Books, Hollywood, Sports, Christmas*, and *Comedy* — all *(abridged)* — all of which are published and/or translated into over a dozen languages. TV credits include recurring roles on *Alias, 24, The Practice, Ally McBeal*, and *Felicity*; and various Guys in Ties on *ER, X-Files, West Wing, Gilmore Girls, Nip/Tuck*, and shows like them. Austin produces and hosts the weekly RSC Podcast, available on iTunes and at ReducedShakespeare.com. Follow him on Twitter *@austintichenor*.

For their contributions to the development
of the script, the authors wish to thank:

Dee Ryan, Adrian Scarborough, Rob Richards, Dominic Conti, Jennifer King, Michael Faulkner, John Tichenor, Andrew Klein, Dr. Catherine Reedy, Jason Feddy, Benedict the Mad, Quincy and Daisy Tichenor, Peter Holland, Samuel Taylor, Elaine Randolph, Alli Bostedt, Campbell and Cian Martin, Jennifer Ruygt, Kate Powers, Grant Mudge, Christopher Moore, Freya Marcelius, Cameo Cinema in St. Helena CA, Ron Severdia and the Shakespeare Pro App, Sonoma Valley High School Drama Department, Dan Saski, Teddy Spencer, Chad Yarish, the late great Howard Ashman, and Jane Martin.

FOR WHAT IT'S WORTH

Although within this published script we use the names of the original cast, your actors should their own names and physical characteristics.

There are a number of topical references in the script. The humour and relevance of some of these will fade over time, so we encourage each production to keep these references as up-to-date as possible. This is not to say that scenes should be re-written (which is, in fact, strictly prohibited) but rather we are giving you permission to change a punchline or reference from "Cumberbatch" to "Ryan Gosling" or some other currently-unknown-but-soon-to-be-discovered-dreamboat.

The production elements described in the script are from the original Reduced Shakespeare Company production. Consequently the scenery, props and costumes were all reduced in both quality and number. We'd encourage you to do the same.

In our experience, the script works best when it is performed simply and seriously. That is to say, the script is funny so play it straight. Play it with the intensity and focus you'd play an actual Shakespeare script. And remember that each character has wildly different feelings about how this should be done, and that if left alone they'd create three wildly different productions. Enjoy that tension and revel in the comedy that conflict can create.

WILLIAM SHAKESPEARE'S LONG LOST FIRST PLAY (ABRIDGED) was first performed by the Reduced Shakespeare Company at The Folger Theatre, Washington DC (Janet Alexander Griffin, Artistic Director), April 21 – May 8, 2016. The cast was: Reed Martin, Teddy Spencer, Austin Tichenor.

With the same cast, the play had its European premiere at the Pleasance Courtyard as part of the Edinburgh Festival Fringe, August 3–29, 2016. The production subsequently toured across the UK, February – May, 2017, with actors Joseph Maudsley, Matthew Pearson and James Percy.

Directed by the authors, the script was workshopped and developed in a non-RSC production at

Shakespeare Napa Valley
St Helena, California
Jennifer King, Artistic Director
June 26 – July 12, 2015

and

Notre Dame Shakespeare Festival
Notre Dame University
South Bend, Indiana
Grant Mudge, Producing Artistic Director
August 4 – 30, 2015

THE CAST

AUSTIN (*An enthusiastic academic*)

REED (*A pragmatic tough guy*)

TEDDY (*A sincere and excited innocent*)

. . . playing, in order of appearance . . .

CHORUS	POMPEY
ANTIPHOLUS	CARDENIO
DROMIO OF SYRACUSE	PERICLES
PUCK	KING LEAR
OBERON	PROSPERO
HOLOFERNES	MARINA
ARIEL	BEAR
HAMLET	CLEOPATRA
LADY MACBETH	RICHARD II
DAUPHIN	KATE
MISTRESS QUICKLY	SYCORAX
SIR JOHN FALSTAFF	GONERIL
PROTEUS	CORDELIA
VALENTINE	REGAN
JULIET	HENRY IV
RICHARD III	HENRY V
BEATRICE	HENRY VIII
1ST WITCH	MALVOLIAGO
2ND WITCH	PETRUCHIO
3RD WITCH	CALIBAN
BOTTOM	JULIUS CAESAR
VIOLA	TIMON OF ATHENS
CESARIO	DROMIO OF EPHESUS

and

WILLIAM SHAKESPEARE

ACT ONE

SCENE ONE: PROLOGUE
(CHORUS)

SETTING: A large Elizabethan drop with two entrances cut into it, right and left of center.

AT RISE: A cloaked hooded figure enters and commands the audience's attention. His face is unseen. He gestures and the house lights go down, then gestures to make a single special rise on him. With a flourish he removes his hood. This is CHORUS.

CHORUS / AUSTIN
O, if a Muse of fire be the food of love, let's eat!
Give me excess of it, a kingdom for a stage,
Princes to act and monarchs to behold the swelling scene!
Can we cram within this wooden 'O'* the very cast
Of witches and wizards and masters and servants
And lovers and fairies and lasses and perverts?
You bet your ass. But pardon, gentles all.
Let us ascend the brightest heaven of invention
And on your imaginary forces work.
Two fairies, both alike in sorcery,
In Fairyland, where we doth lay our play,
From ancient grudge break to new rivalry,
Where magic scary gets carried away.
From forth their frisky fingers, these fairies
Fatally foully confuse friends and foes;
The lover is crowned, royalty marries –
And how we accomplish it, no one knows.
For 'tis your thoughts that now must deck our kings,
Carry them here and there, jumping o'er times,

---

* Unless your theatre is a replica of Shakespeare's Globe, "wooden
'O'" should be changed to reflect your performance space (i.e. "wooden
O, what a beautiful re-creation!" Or "wooden O, what a converted
gymnasium!" Or "wooden O, what a painted backdrop!")

Turning the accomplishment of many years
Into an hour glass, and every place on the globe
Within the girdle of these walls confined:
Six mighty monarchies, eight pairs of twins,
Dysfunctional lovers, unpardonable sins,
Fairies and sprites full of shapes and fancy,
Men in dresses and women so pantsy,
And oceans and forests and shipwrecks and tempests
And spirits of love and regret and rage
Are the *one hundred hours'* traffic of our stage.
Admit me – Chorus – to this mystery;
Who prologue-like your humble patience pray,
Gently to hear – *and loudly enjoy* – our play!

(*He bows.*)

SCENE TWO: INTRODUCTIONS
(AUSTIN, REED, TEDDY)

REED *and* TEDDY *enter and join* AUSTIN, *who ditches his cloak.*

REED	Thank you! Ladies and gentleman, that is the first time that speech has been heard by any audience, anywhere. Good evening/ afternoon, I'm Reed Martin –
TEDDY	I'm Teddy Spencer –
AUSTIN	I'm Austin Tichenor.
REED	And before we get started: First of all, please turn off all electronic devices: phones, hearing aids, pacemakers.
AUSTIN	Also: Please locate the exit nearest your seat. In the event of a fire, please exit the building *before* tweeting about it.

TEDDY   Photography of any kind is not allowed during tonight's performance; it's not only illegal, it's just plain rude. And this theatre is [*or isn't*] equipped with hearing loops so – (*He mouths and pantomimes some words no one can hear.*) That information could save your life.

AUSTIN   Now then. We have made an incredible discovery.

REED   We were on tour in England last year, and we had just finished performing at a theatre in Leicester.

TEDDY   And we went back to Titus, which was parked in a par –

REED   Wait, you should explain what Titus is.

TEDDY   Oh, right. We travel in a large twelve-seat passenger van we call Titus Vandronicus. I know, it's awesome.

AUSTIN   Anyway, we went back to Titus, which was parked in a parking lot in Leicester.

REED   And we saw this hole. In the parking lot.

AUSTIN   And down *in* the hole, we found a pile of bones.

REED   They looked totally unimportant.

AUSTIN   But next to the bones was a bundle of papers.

TEDDY   And the bundle of papers turned out to be – hang on, I'll get it –

(*He exits.*)

AUSTIN   Ladies and gentlemen, that bundle of papers
                turned out to be the most important literary
                discovery of the last four hundred years.

REED   We discovered –

ALL   (*as* TEDDY *enters with it*) William
                Shakespeare's long lost first play!

AUSTIN   Now, we have had this checked and verified.
                There are six surviving examples of
                Shakespeare's handwriting. This is clearly
                written in *all six* of Shakespeare's hands.

TEDDY   This is his actual handwriting!

REED   And we brought it to the Folger Shakespeare
                Library in Washington DC, which holds the
                largest collection of Shakespeare crap in
                the world. And as they were showing us the
                exit, they assured us that this was unlike
                anything they have in their collection.

AUSTIN   But it's not a folio.

REED   No. It's like a fake folio.

TEDDY   Yeah, it's a *faux*-lio!

AUSTIN / REED   Nice.

REED   And it's massive. It's like a double-quarto.

AUSTIN   Scholars call a double-quarto an ocho.

TEDDY   Or a quarto-pounder.

AUSTIN   That's right. And what I love about
            Shakespeare's first play is that it contains
            most of the famous characters and famous
            lines we all know from his later plays.

REED   But they're all woven together into a brand-
            new four hundred year old story line.

TEDDY   Evidence suggests he was only seventeen
            years old when he wrote this!

AUSTIN   And what you just heard is the opening
            prologue to this epic work, which means
            it's probably the first speech Shakespeare
            ever wrote. It's like the opening speeches of
            Romeo and Juliet, *Twelfth Night*, and *Henry
            V* – but so much less good!

TEDDY   This is the first draft of literary history!

AUSTIN   You can tell he didn't even know what to
            call it. Here on the cover is a list of titles
            Shakespeare was considering . . . *West Side
            Story* –

TEDDY   *One Hundred and One Venetians* –

AUSTIN   *Richard Four: The Revengening* –

REED   *Game of Thrones* –

TEDDY   *Romeo and Ethel, the Pirate's Daughter* –

AUSTIN   Good title. *The Only Way Is Verona* [*or The
            Real Merry Housewives of Windsor*] –

REED   *Breaking Bard* –

AUSTIN   *Much Ado About Something Quite
            Important, Really* –

TEDDY   And –

ALL   *Hamilton* [*Or whatever the biggest most
               well-known stage production currently is*].

REED   Well, whatever he intended to call it, tonight
               ladies and gentlemen, we will perform
               for the first time anywhere in the history
               of ever, the world premiere of William
               Shakespeare's Long Lost First Play.

               (REED *and* AUSTIN *start to go.*)

TEDDY   That's right! Just as soon as the rest of the
               actors get here, we'll attempt a feat that has
               never –

REED   Woah, wait a second.

AUSTIN   Teddy, there are no other actors.

REED   There's just the three of us.

TEDDY   Are you shitting me?

REED   No.

TEDDY   What about Dame Judi Dench? Or Lenny
               Henry V or Benedict Bumbercatch [*Or three
               other actors your audience will recognise*]?
               Aren't they coming?

REED   No.

AUSTIN   It's just us.

TEDDY   We can't do this by ourselves!

REED   Of course we can.

TEDDY   No, we can't! (*Pointing to the manuscript.*)
                 Look at the cast list. There's one thousand,
                 six hundred and thirty-nine characters in
                 here!

AUSTIN   The three of us can do that.

REED   Easily. Besides, I've made some cuts.

AUSTIN   Wait, what?

REED   Yeah, we gotta be out of here in two hours.

AUSTIN   No, no, no, we've got to perform this
                 whole masterpiece. We have a literary
                 responsibility!

REED   No, we have a theatrical opportunity! And
                 uncut this thing is over a hundred hours
                 long.

AUSTIN   Yeah, I don't know . . .

TEDDY   It doesn't matter. We're still gonna need
                 more people!

REED   No, don't say – !!

AUSTIN
(*in full Shakespearean bombast*) What's he that wishes so?
The fewer men, the greater share of honour.
God's will! I pray thee, wish not one man more.

REED   (*to* TEDDY) See what you did?

AUSTIN
And he which hath no stomach to this fight,
Let him depart; his passport shall be made,
And crowns for convoy put into his purse;
We would not act in that man's company.

TEDDY   I'm sorry.

REED   (*to* TEDDY) Will you just do it?

AUSTIN
Come along then, my two noble kinsmen,
For thespians in England now-a-bed
Shall think themselves accurs'd they were not here,
And they will hold their manhoods cheap –

TEDDY   I am *not* holding my manhood cheap.

REED   I'm not holding your manhood at all.

AUSTIN
And rue the day they did not with us perform –

ALL
– William Shakespeare's Long Lost First Play!

                   (AUSTIN *and* TEDDY *exit as* REED *says* . . .)

REED   Abridged!

                   (REED *plays "Greensleeves" on a kazoo,*
                   or recorder, or both. As ANTIPHOLUS *and*
                   DROMIO *enter,* REED *plays the familiar*
                   "Shave and a haircut, two bits" music on
                   his instrument and quickly exits.)

                   SCENE THREE: ACT ONE, 1
           (ANTIPHOLUS, DROMIO, PUCK, REED, OBERON)

ANTIPHOLUS *and* DROMIO, *both of Syracuse, enter.*

ANTIPHOLUS / AUSTIN
'Tis I, Antipholus, the rich and brave.

DROMIO / TEDDY
And I, called Dromio, this big-shot's slave.

ANTIPHOLUS / AUSTIN
In Syracuse was I born, with a brother
Who, both of us each so like the other
We could not be distinguished but by names.

DROMIO / TEDDY
And my tale and story are both the sames!
For in that hour, and in the same inn,
My mother gave birth to me and *my* twin!
Yet since my parents were exceedingly poor
We were sold and brought up to attend your
Wishes and desires.

ANTIPHOLUS / AUSTIN
                         All was well until
My father, a merchant, with time to kill
Decided to sail, and felt so secure
He brought us all on a three-hour tour.

DROMIO / TEDDY
The weather started getting rough.

ANTIPHOLUS / AUSTIN
The tiny ship was tossed
Despite the courage of the fearless crew

BOTH
Our brothers both were lost.

ANTIPHOLUS / AUSTIN
Now, at eighteen years, I'm inquisitive
And my attendant, whose case is so like –

DROMIO / TEDDY
Not!

ANTIPHOLUS / AUSTIN
Joins me now here in Ephesus,
Hopeless to find, yet loath to leave unsought
The brother I lost –

DROMIO / TEDDY
                    – and the brother your mother bought!

                    (*The characters freeze.* REED *steps forward.*)

REED   Okay. So far so what. Shakespeare begins
                    his long lost first play the same way he'd
                    later begin his first publicly-performed play,
                    The Comedy of Errors: With Antipholus
                    and Dromio searching for their long lost
                    twins. But now, into this farcical world
                    of shipwrecks and mistaken identity,
                    Shakespeare introduces characters familiar
                    to us from his other plays, beginning
                    with a magical creature we know from *A
                    Midsummer Night's Dream.*

                    (*He puts on short devil's horns and becomes
                    the mischievous sprite Robin Goodfellow,
                    commonly known as* PUCK.)

PUCK / REED
What Syracusans have I come upon?

                    (*Going into the audience to watch the actors.*)

Be they good models to build mischief on?

DROMIO / TEDDY
(*consulting a map; to the audience*)
Excuse me, sir/ma'am, we're on our last legs.
Canst thou direct us to the nearest Greggs?*

ANTIPHOLUS / AUSTIN
Go bear this to the Boar's Head Tavern, where we host,
And stay there, Dromio, till I come to thee:
A trusty villain, sir, that very oft,

---

* *Update this couplet for a restaurant near you.*

When I am dull with care and melancholy,
Lighten my humor with your merry jests.

(*Kicking him away.*)

Now get thee away.

DROMIO / TEDDY
Was there ever any man thus beaten out of season,
When in the why and the wherefore is neither rhyme nor reason?

(*He exits.* PUCK *calls to* ANTIPHOLUS, *and
begins to climb over audience members.*)

PUCK / REED
How now, sirrah! Whither wander I?
Over hill, over Dale –

(*To an audience membe*r) Sorry, Dale.

Through bush, through brier,
Over park, over Gail –

(*Flirty to an audience member.*) What's up,
Gail?

Through flood, through fire
Swifter than the moon's sphere –
Tell me, what is it that bringeth you here?

ANTIPHOLUS / AUSTIN
I to the world am like a drop of water
That in the ocean seeks another drip.
So I, to find a mother and a brother,
In quest of them, unhappy, lose myself.

PUCK / REED
Lose thyself, eh? What an intriguing thought.
Let's see, to where has your simple friend got?

> (PUCK *gestures and magically pulls* DROMIO
> *back on stage. The sound of wind-chimes*
> *accompanies this gesture.*)

ANTIPHOLUS / AUSTIN
What, art thou a fairy? Art thou a sprite?

PUCK / REED
Call you me fairy? Thou speakest aright.
I am that merry wanderer of the night
Called Robin Goodfellow. You are in luck!
Some call me 'Hobgoblin' or just sweet Puck.

DROMIO / TEDDY
(*freaking out and running around*)
This is the fairy land! O spite of spites!
We talk with goblins, owls, and sprites – !

> (PUCK *freezes him.*)

PUCK / REED
I serve the Fairy King in th'Athenian wood
But that I cometh here is best and good.
For Oberon is passing fell and wrath –

> (DROMIO *unfreezes and continues his freak-*
> *out.*)

DROMIO / TEDDY
And under their dark spell we fallen hath!
If we obey them not, this will ensue:
They'll suck our breath or pinch us –

> (PUCK *freezes him again.*)

PUCK / REED   Quiet, you.

ANTIPHOLUS / AUSTIN
They say this town is full of deception
With soul-killing witches that deceive the eye –

PUCK / REED
Not witches so much as it is just I!

(*Freezing* ANTIPHOLUS.)

You Antipholus and you Dromio
I transport you now to Italy – Go!

(PUCK *sends them magically offstage; more chimes.*)

Now am I free until my master calls!

OBERON / AUSTIN (*off stage*)
Robin! My gentle Puck, come hither!

PUCK / REED   Balls.

(*He exits.*)

SCENE FOUR: INTERJECTION
(HOLOFERNES, REED, AUSTIN)

AUSTIN *enters as elderly* HOLOFERNES, *dressed in academic robes and wearing glasses.*

HOLOFERNES / AUSTIN
Most barbarous intimation! Yet a kind of
insinuation, as 'twere, in via, in way, of explication –

REED   (*entering still dressed as* PUCK) Woah, stop.
                I've cut Holofernes.

AUSTIN   What?

REED   Yeah, I've cut all of Shakespeare's pompous
                annoying blabbermouths: Polonius, Egeon,
                Pandarus, Justice Shallow –

AUSTIN   Wait, we need at least one pompous annoying windbag.

REED   We've got you.

AUSTIN   That's true.

REED   I also cut Shakespeare's examination of the effects of sleep deprivation on the monarchy.

AUSTIN   *Pericles, The Prince Is Tired?*

REED   It's cut.

AUSTIN   What about *Cymbeline?*

REED   Cut.

AUSTIN   *Coriolanus?*

REED   Cut.

AUSTIN   *Love's Labours?*

REED   Lost.

AUSTIN   Why?

REED   *Love's Labours* is a long story, and as in *Henry The Eighth*, Shakespeare doesn't tell it very well.

AUSTIN   (*exiting*) Argh. This is gonna be a long night.

REED   Not any more. In fact, you know what – (*Calling offstage.*) Teddy?

TEDDY   (*off*) Yeah?

REED   We're skipping ahead!

TEDDY   (*off*) Where to?

REED   Act One, Scene Thirty-Eight!

TEDDY   (*off*) Sweet!

REED   In which Puck finally comes face to face
                with his sworn mortal enemy.

                (*He puts his horns back on and begins the
                next scene.*)

SCENE FIVE: ACT ONE, 38
(PUCK, ARIEL, REED, TEDDY, AUSTIN, HAMLET, LADY MACBETH)

PUCK / REED
Now then, of Dromio I must hear tell –

                (*Wind chimes.*)

Wait! 'Tis the sprite I love least, Ariel!

                (*The airy spirit* ARIEL *enters, dressed in a
                mermaid's costume: long red wig, clamshell
                bra, and fish tail over her feet. She hops on
                clumsily.*)

PUCK / REED
How now, spirit, whither – ?

                (*Breaking character.*) What are you doing?

TEDDY   What does it look like? I'm playing Ariel.

REED   Disney's Ariel?

TEDDY   Uh, yeah! Shakespeare's greatest creation is
                 Ariel, the little mermaid.

AUSTIN   (*having re-entered to witness this travesty*)
                 Woah, woah! Shakespeare's Ariel is not a
                 Disney character.

TEDDY   Are you kidding? *All* Disney movies are
                 based on Shakespeare!

AUSTIN   No, they're not! What's the Disney version
                 of *Hamlet*, where the prince's father is
                 murdered by his uncle?

TEDDY   *The Lion King.*

AUSTIN   That's a bad example. What about *Henry
                 IV, Part 1*, where a young man shirks his
                 responsibilities with his fat, lazy friend?

TEDDY   *The Jungle Book.*

AUSTIN   What?

TEDDY   Mowgli and Baloo.

REED   So what's the Disney version of *King John?*

TEDDY   *Pete's Dragon.*

REED   Nobody's seen *Pete's Dragon.*

TEDDY   Nobody's seen *King John.*

AUSTIN   What about *Richard the Third?*

TEDDY   *Hunchback of Notre Dame.*

REED   *Midsummer Night's Dream?*

TEDDY   *Fantasia.* Magic run amok.

AUSTIN   *Macbeth.*

TEDDY   *The Black Cauldron.*

REED   *Comedy of Errors.*

TEDDY   *The Parent Trap!*

REED   What?

TEDDY   Long lost identical twins!

AUSTIN   *Othello.*

TEDDY   *Othello* is the basis of *Aladdin.*

AUSTIN   No, it isn't.

TEDDY   What's the parrot's name?

AUSTIN   Iago. Damn. What about *The Tempest?*

TEDDY   *Swiss Family Robinson.*

AUSTIN   Okay, *Merchant of Venice.*

TEDDY   Isn't that full of offensive racial
             stereotypes?

AUSTIN   Yup.

TEDDY   *Song of the South!*

REED   So what's the Disney version of *Winter's
             Tale?*

TEDDY   *Frozen.*

REED   But . . .

TEDDY   Let it go.

REED   Teddy, I don't think . . .

TEDDY   LET IT GO!

AUSTIN   Yeah, I'm not buying this.

REED   No, Austin, I think Teddy's right.

AUSTIN   What?

REED   If you think about it, Walt Disney was the modern-day Shakespeare.

AUSTIN   (*together*) No, he wasn't!

TEDDY   (*together*) Yes!

REED   He became ridiculously rich by rewriting history and stealing existing stories and making them his own.

AUSTIN   Who, Disney or Shakespeare?

REED / TEDDY   Yes!

REED   And have you been to Stratford-Upon-Avon recently? They should rename it Shakespeareland.

TEDDY   (*singing*) S - H - A –

REED   A for Amazing genius.

TEDDY   (*singing*) K - E - S –

REED   S for Super Savvy businessman.

TEDDY / REED   (*singing*) P - E - A - R - E!

AUSTIN   E for Idiotic! Irregardless, Shakespeare's
                  Ariel is not a mermaid!

TEDDY   All right. I can't walk in this anyway.

REED   Okay, come in again.

                  (AUSTIN *and* TEDDY *exit.* PUCK *re-starts the
                  scene.*)

PUCK / REED
Now then, of Dromio –

TEDDY   (*off*) Wait!

AUSTIN   (*sticking his head on*) He's got his flipper
                  caught in his zipper.

REED   Wouldn't be the first time. (*As* PUCK.) Okay?

TEDDY   (*off*) Okay.

PUCK / REED
Now then, of Dromio I must hear tell –

                  (*Wind chimes.*)

Wait! 'Tis the sprite I love least, Ariel!

                  (ARIEL *enters again, this time with no tail.*)

PUCK / REED
How now, spirit, whither wander you?

ARIEL / TEDDY
I fly, I swim, I dive under the sea,
Under the sea, darling it's better down
Where it's wetter, take it from me!

(AUSTIN *steps out, shakes his head, and exits*.)

ARIEL / TEDDY
Either I mistake your shape and making quite
Or else you are that shrewd and knavish sprite
Robin Goodfellow, my sworn enemy.

PUCK / REED
My dear Fairy Disdain. Are you yet living?

ARIEL / TEDDY
(*aside*) There is a kind of merry war betwixt us.

PUCK / REED
(*aside*) We never meet but there's a skirmish of wit between us.
Ariel, thou'st never told me
Exactly what occasions thy jealousy?

ARIEL / TEDDY
Thou knowst what thou did.

PUCK / REED
When we were young, you were my bestest friend.

ARIEL / TEDDY
Yes, which your treachery brought to an end!
Besides, I say and will in magic prove
That all your treasons for these many years . . .

PUCK / REED
I do protest I never injured thee
But love thee better than thou canst devise!

ARIEL / TEDDY
Wandering free, not wishing to be
Part of your world, I thus happened to see
Those two simple Greeks who, you rapscallion,
You sent off and turned into Eye-talians.
I knew right away that something was up.
What plans now pour from your most puckish cup?

PUCK / REED
Mere merry mischief, my magical mate.

ARIEL / TEDDY
Whether it's mischief is up for debate.

PUCK / REED
I sent them on a merry adventure!

ARIEL / TEDDY
Dost thou serve at thy master's indenture?

PUCK / REED
No. I hope their confusion lasts longer.

ARIEL / TEDDY
And dost thou think thy power is stronger
Than mine?

PUCK / REED
            I am quite a master of japes.

ARIEL / TEDDY
Well, thou knows that *I'm* a shifter of shapes!
I can look like *this*, or –

> (*He leaps in one door.* AUSTIN *leaps out the
> other, dressed identically.* AUSTIN *mouths
> the words as* TEDDY *says them offstage.*)

ARIEL / TEDDY (*cont'd, off*)
                        – Like *this!*

> (AUSTIN *leaps off.* TEDDY *leaps on through
> the other doorway.*)

ARIEL / TEDDY
I speak in many voices –

> (*She mouths as* AUSTIN *says* . . .)

AUSTIN / ARIEL (*2nd, off*)
                 – all of them strong!

PUCK / REED
I think we can prove who's stronger 'ere long.

ARIEL / TEDDY
But how can we prove who is the greater?

PUCK / REED
I'll put a girdle round the earth. Later!

                (PUCK *exits and re-enters immediately with*
                the melancholy prince of Denmark, HAMLET.
                Wind chimes.)

PUCK / REED
I'm so sorry. That took forever!
But I found this sad man who can never
Make his mind up or make a decision.

ARIEL / TEDDY
What's his name?

PUCK / REED
                 Hamlet. Shh! Let us listen –

HAMLET / AUSTIN
To be, or not to be, that is the question:
Whether 'tis nobler in the mind to suffer
The slings and arrows of outrageous fortune,
Or to take arms against a sea of troubles,
And by opposing, end them.

                (ARIEL *waves her hand.* HAMLET *freezes.*)

ARIEL / TEDDY
                 Please. End *this*.
It's like he needs a hand-hold, a guide.

PUCK / REED
No matter the topic he can't decide.
This poor, reflective, indecisive boy
I present to you as a lovely toy!

ARIEL / TEDDY
I need no presents, especially from you.

PUCK / REED
But look at all the fun things you can do!

> (PUCK *places a tiny wig on the skull* HAMLET
> *holds and unfreezes him.*)

HAMLET / AUSTIN
Toupee, or not toupee –

> (*He gestures again.* HAMLET *freezes and*
> PUCK *replaces the skull and toupee with*
> *a Starbucks cup. He gestures again and*
> HAMLET *unfreezes.*)

HAMLET / AUSTIN
Latte, or not latte –

> (*Now* ARIEL *gestures and magically gives*
> HAMLET *a toy saxophone. She gestures again*
> *and* HAMLET *unfreezes.*)

HAMLET / AUSTIN
Tuba, or not tuba, that is a saxophone.

> (PUCK *gestures and hands* HAMLET *a joint.*
> *Unfreezes.*)

HAMLET / AUSTIN
Doobie, or not doobie –

> (*Puff.*)

– that –

>   (PUCK *gestures, grabs the joint and*
>   *unfreezes* HAMLET *in a new direction.*)

HAMLET / AUSTIN
(*singing*) *Doobie-doobie-do,* that is the Sinatra –

>   (ARIEL *gestures him in a different direction.*)

HAMLET / AUSTIN
Ser o no ser, that is the Spanish.

>   (PUCK *gestures.*)

HAMLET / AUSTIN
Ikirubeki ka shinubeki ka, that is the Japanese.

>   (ARIEL *gestures.*)

HAMLET / AUSTIN
Ootay eebay, oryay otnay ootay eebay,
atthay isyay eethay igPay atinLay.
Ut-way ee-thay uck-fay?!

>   (ARIEL *and* PUCK *both gesture.* HAMLET
>   *freezes. They laugh, delighted at their*
>   *mischief, then stop, embarrassed at being in*
>   *agreement.*)

PUCK / REED
I tire of this game. I leave him for you
To do with whatever you want to do.

ARIEL / TEDDY
God be with you. Let's meet as little as we can.

PUCK / REED (*exiting*)
I do desire we may be better strangers! TTFN!

ARIEL / TEDDY
(*frustrated; re.* HAMLET)

What do I do with this wavering guy?
He must *make a choice* – or least of all try.
Someone must help him. I have it! I'll show
Him a young striver in Scotland I know.
She wants a crown and's so eager to win it
They'll be engaged in less than a minute.
She's the best teacher who ever drew breath:
That mean motivator, Lady Macbeth!

> (ARIEL *conjures* LADY MACBETH: *an intense
> femme fatale.* ARIEL *leaves.*)

LADY MACBETH / REED
Worthy Hamlet! Dane of Cawdor!

HAMLET / AUSTIN
                            Good lady,
In thy orisons be all my sins remembered.

LADY MACBETH / REED
How fares our fiancé Hamlet?

HAMLET / AUSTIN
I'm sorry, when did we become betrothed?

LADY MACBETH / REED
Don't you remember? Have you an antic disposition?

HAMLET / AUSTIN
No, I am but mad north-northwest, I know
A hawk from a handsaw.

LADY MACBETH
Yeah, that's tough.

HAMLET / AUSTIN
The serpent that did sting my father's life now wears his crown!
I know that I needs must with wings as swift
As meditation sweep to my revenge.

LADY MACBETH / REED
Swift as *meditation?* We'll be here all night.
Why seems revenge so difficult with thee?

HAMLET / AUSTIN
"Seems", madam? Nay, it is. I know not "seems".
But in that sleep of death what dreams may come
When he has shuffled off this mortal coil
Must give us pause.

LADY MACBETH
                    No, no pausing, Hamlet!
Canst thou not slay him while he's at prayer?

HAMLET / AUSTIN
So he goes to heaven? No. He took my father grossly.

LADY MACBETH
You tend to be a 'not to be' Hamlet;
I need you to be a 'to *be*' Hamlet!
(*Grabbing him.*) Prince thou art and the king thou shalt be.
I want to be queen and go to Niagara
So you need to find some mental viagra!

HAMLET / AUSTIN
                    Prithee, peace.
I dare do all that may become a man.
Who dares more?

LADY MACBETH / REED
I have given suck, and know
How tender 'tis to love the babe that milks me.
I would, while it was smiling in my face,
Have plucked my nipple from his boneless gums
And dashed his brains out.

HAMLET / AUSTIN
                    Holy crap. If we fail –

LADY MACBETH / REED
(*grabbing his crotch*)
Screw your courage to the sticking place
And we'll not fail.

HAMLET / AUSTIN
(*high-pitched voice*)   All right. I am settled.

> (*She lets him go and exits.* HAMLET *follows her.*)

HAMLET / AUSTIN
(*as he hobbles off*) Screw my sticky to the what now?

> (*He exits.*)

SCENE SIX: INTERJECTION
(DAUPHIN, TEDDY, REED, AUSTIN)

Teddy enters, making dolphin sounds. REED *re-enters, still wearing his* LADY M *dress but holding the wig.*

REED	Stop, stop, stop! What are you doing?
TEDDY	I'm playing the Dolphin.
REED	It's pronounced Dauphin.
TEDDY	I know. I'm doing it on porpoise.
REED	Stop it! The Dauphin's been cut.
TEDDY	I know! You've cut like ninety-nine percent of the play.
REED	(*showing him the list of cuts*) Yes! Otherwise, it's four days long! Haven't you been listening?

TEDDY   Wait a minute! You cut the old Italian wood
               carver and his puppet?

REED   Gepetto and Petruchio? Yes! Most of it.

AUSTIN   (*entering with the manuscript*) What's going
               on?

TEDDY   He's cutting all my favorite parts. (*He exits.*)

AUSTIN   Tell me about it. You're also cutting some
               of my favorite first-draft versions of
               Shakespeare's most iconic lines.

REED   Like what?

AUSTIN   Like "Beware the Ides of February"!

REED   So?

AUSTIN   Or what about Polonius's line, "The
               important thing about brevity is that the use
               of it can frequently take the appearance if
               not the substance of the soul of wit."

REED   There's a reason he rewrote that.

AUSTIN   Or when Hamlet says, "Oh, that this too too
               salad fresh were a tuna melt."

REED   NO!

AUSTIN   Then how is the audience going to know
               about Hamlet's edible complex?

REED   They don't need to.

AUSTIN   Then at least let me read this one speech
               for you. It's very short. The best way to

	appreciate Shakespeare's language, his poetry, is to read it.
REED	Fine.
	(AUSTIN *opens the manuscript and very deliberately clears his throat. Then he begins to read – silently.*)
REED	(*after a beat*) Whenever you're ready.
AUSTIN	I'm done. Now you read it.
REED	No! This play was created to be performed, not read! Let's go!
AUSTIN	(*as he exits*) Hey, this stuff is interesting to all the Shakespeare scholars here tonight!
REED	Yeah, both of them love it. (*To the audience.*) Now, we come finally to the top of Shakespeare's Act Two, in which the competition between Puck and Ariel is just heating up, and we arrive at the Boar's Head Tavern to see what happened to the gold that Dromio brought there . . .
	(*He exits.*)

SCENE SEVEN: ACT TWO, 54
(MISTRESS QUICKLY, FALSTAFF, ARIEL, PUCK)

MISTRESS QUICKLY *enters, Cockney hostess of the Boar's Head Tavern.*

QUICKLY / TED.	Where is he? Where is that huge bombard of sack, that stuffed cloakbag of guts, that roasted ox with the pudding in his belly, Sir John Falstaff?

(SIR JOHN FALSTAFF *enters, boldly and
drunkenly. He has wild red hair and beard
and is enormously fat.*)

FALST. / AUST.   A whore! A whore! My kingdom for a
                 whore!

QUICKLY / TED.   There you are, thou claybrained guts, thou
                 knotty-pated fool, thou whoreson, obscene,
                 greasy tallow catch!

FALST. / AUST.   Ah, and is not my hostess of the tavern a
                 most sweet wench?

QUICKLY / TED.   None of your flattery, Sir John. There's
                 neither honesty, manhood, nor good
                 fellowship in thee.

FALST. / AUST.   What, are thou mad? Give us a cup of sack,
                 woman!

QUICKLY / TED.   You owe me money, Sir John!

FALST. / AUST.   You lie, Hostess, and I'll be sworn my
                 pocket was picked last night!

QUICKLY / TED.   Why, Sir John, what do you think, Sir John,
                 that I keep thieves in my house?

FALST. / AUST.   Go to, I know you well enough!

QUICKLY / TED.   No, Sir John, you do not know me, Sir John.
                 I know you, Sir John. You owe me money,
                 Sir John, and now you pick a quarrel to
                 beguile me of it!

FALST. / AUST.   Peace, good pint-pot. Peace, good tickle-
                 brain.

QUICKLY / TED.   You hath eaten me out of house and home, and put all my substance into that fat belly of yours. But I will have some of it out again, or I will banish you from the Boar's Head!

FALST. / AUST.   No, my good lady, banish Caesar, banish Prince Hal, but for sweet Jack Falstaff, kind Jack Falstaff – (*Struggling to his knees.*) – true Jack Falstaff, banish not him thy lady's company. Banish plump Jack and banish all the world.

(*He belches. Or farts. Or both.*)

QUICKLY / TED.   You owe money here besides, money lent you, four-and-twenty pound!

(*She exits. He calls after her.*)

FALST. / AUST.   That's right, begone, Mistress Quickly! And bring me a cup of sack! My means are very slender but my waist is great. I would it were otherwise.

(*As* FALSTAFF *struggles to raise his bulk off the floor,* ARIEL *enters and hovers. We hear wind chimes.*)

ARIEL / TEDDY
Dromio did as Antipholus commands:
Brought the gold here which satisfies my plans.
So now for reasons no one understands,
I'll place Dromio's gold in Falstaff's hands.

(*She does, and exits.*)

FALST. / AUST.
(*sensing a magical presence*) By this fire, that's God's angel!

(*Looking in the bag.*) 'Tis a purse of gold most resolutely
snatch'd!

>   (QUICKLY *makes a frustrated sobbing noise
>   offstage.*)

FALST. / AUST.
My hostess hast called me to a reckoning. Pay her.

>   (*He starts to go.*)

QUICKLY   (*off*) I'll kill the fat bastard!

FALST. / AUST.   Or – buy barrels of sack. The better part of
                  valor is discretion; I must take this purse
                  and go!

>   (*He runs off.* PUCK *enters to see him go.*)

PUCK / REED
What's Ariel done, that impudent sprite?
Is there method to her madness this night?
She will not surpass me without a fight,
But first, I must see if Dromio's all right.

>   (*He exits.*)

                    SCENE EIGHT: ACT TWO, 55
               (DROMIO, JULIET, PROTEUS, VALENTINE,
                     PUCK, RICHARD, BEATRICE)

DROMIO *runs on, not knowing where he is.*

DROMIO / TEDDY Woah . . . what is this place? How have I
                come so far?

> (*Two gentlemen of Verona enter:* PROTEUS *and* VALENTINE. *They speak as they cross and exit.*)

PROTEUS / REED
Two gentlemen of Verona we are,
Valentine!

VALENTINE / AUSTIN
          Proteus, don't grieve.
Verona, for a while I take my leave [*of you*]
To visit friends in –

> (*They exit.* DROMIO *realizes where he is.*)

DROMIO / TEDDY
'Tis fair Verona where we lay our scene!

> (PUCK *enters and freezes* DROMIO.)

PUCK / REED
Oh, the poor fellow's alone in this world.
I should show him a Verona home girl.
Juliet will help him to do as he pleases
And immediately like what she sees-es.

> (*He gestures and* JULIET CAPULET *enters.* PUCK *holds up a purple flower.*)

PUCK / REED
The juice of this flower on eyelids laid
Will make this woman madly dote upon
Whatever next live creature that she sees.
(*Casting a spell.*) What thou seest when thou dost wake,
Do it for thy true love take.
You're looking so crazy in love
Got you looking, got you looking so crazy in love

PUCK / REED & JULIET / AUSTIN
Uh oh, uh oh, uh oh, oh no no!

(PUCK *sits in the audience as* JULIET *snaps
to, sees* DROMIO, *and is instantly smitten.
All of her lines snap back and forth between
sweetly loving and obsessively intense.*)

JULIET / AUSTIN
(*sweet*) O, he doth teach the torches to burn bright!
(*intense*) I am crazy in love, love at first sight,
For I ne'er saw –
(*sweet*) true beauty till this night.

DROMIO / TEDDY
(*looking around*) Dost thou mean me? My name is Dromio –

JULIET / AUSTIN
(*sweet*) O Dromio, Dromio, wherefore art thou, Dromio?

DROMIO / TEDDY
(*confused*) I'm right here . . .

JULIET / AUSTIN
No . . . I mean . . .
(*intense*) *Why* art thou called Dromio?

DROMIO / TEDDY
Not sure. My brother's name is Dromio too –
Which makes no sense now that I think of it.

JULIET / AUSTIN
(*sweet*) What's in a name? No matter, I love it!
(*intense*) Dost thou love me?

DROMIO / TEDDY
I –

JULIET / AUSTIN
(*sweet*) I knew thou would say 'Ay'!
And I will take thy word. My heart's dear love –

DROMIO / TEDDY
(*backing away*) This is too rash, too unadvised, too sudden –

JULIET / AUSTIN
(*intense*) O wilt thou leave me so unsatisfied?

DROMIO / TEDDY
What satisfaction canst thou have tonight?

JULIET / AUSTIN
(*sweet*) Th'exchange of thy love's faithful vow for mine!

DROMIO / TEDDY
As from a bear a man would run for life,
So fly I from her that would be my wife!

(*He runs off, with* JULIET *in hot pursuit.*)

JULIET / AUSTIN
(*as she goes*) No! Don't go! Parting is such –
(*intense*) Sweet sorrow!
(*exiting after him*) Oh no no!

(PUCK'S *delighted at what he hath wrought.*)

PUCK / REED
(*gleefully*) Never was there a story of more woe
Than this of Juliet and her Dromio!
But clearly now I must step up my game
Ariel's meddling doth make me look lame.
I can help people! I too can be strong!
In fact, I know just the person. A long
Ways away, to England I will now go –

(*He takes a tiny step to the right and lands
in England. He wipes his brow.*)

PUCK / REED
To find the friendliest person I know.
A lovelorn Duke for whom romance is rare

Because he cannot flatter and look fair.
I'll find him a mate and I'll be brand new:
Not just mischievous Puck; noble Puck too.
He hath the finest feelings you foster:
I give to thee Richard, Duke of Gloucester!

>   (PUCK *gestures and* RICHARD III *limps on,*
>   *hunchbacked with the classic pageboy. He's*
>   *the nicest guy imaginable.*)

RICHARD / AUSTIN
Now is the winter of our discontent
Made glorious summer by this son of York.
For I, that am not shaped for sportive tricks,
Nor made to court an amorous looking glass;
I, that am rudely stamped and want love's majesty
To strut before a wanton ambling nymph;
And am so lame and unfashionable
That dogs bark at me as I halt by them.

>   (PUCK *barks twice.*)

RICHARD / AUSTIN
See?

>   (PUCK *freezes* RICHARD.)

PUCK / REED
Look at him, cooing, alone as a dove,
With a hump only a mother could love.
He's so soft, like a pair of wool mittens,
He loves babies and puppies and kittens!
True, he's misshapen, which helpeth him not;
Women can't see all the fine wit he's got.
For him I shall bring to this arena
One witty woman: Beatrice of Messina.

>   (PUCK *gestures and* RICHARD *unfreezes.*
>   BEATRICE *enters, calling to someone*
>   *offstage.*)

BEATRICE / TEDDY
Yeah? Kiss this!

> (RICHARD'S *like a love-struck schoolboy,*
> *not at all the Machiavellian manipulator he*
> *usually is.* PUCK *watches.*)

RICHARD / AUSTIN
(*aside*) By this day, she's a fair lady.
I do spy some marks of love in her.
(*to* BEATRICE) Your beauty, it will haunt me in my sleep.
Might I live one hour in your sweet bosom?

BEATRICE / TEDDY
I will not desire that.

RICHARD / AUSTIN
That hurts. If you prick me, do I not bleed?

BEATRICE / TEDDY
You talk of pricks?!

RICHARD / AUSTIN
Yes, but –

BEATRICE / TEDDY
You wicked man!

RICHARD / AUSTIN
Is there any way to show you friendship?

BEATRICE / TEDDY
Begone, defused infection of a man.

RICHARD / AUSTIN
Come come, you wasp; i'faith, you are too angry.

BEATRICE / TEDDY
If I be waspish best beware my sting.

RICHARD / AUSTIN
My remedy then is to pluck it out.

BEATRICE / TEDDY
Ay, if the fool could find it where it lies.

RICHARD / AUSTIN
Who knows not where a wasp does wear his sting? In his tail.

BEATRICE / TEDDY
In his tongue.

RICHARD / AUSTIN
Whose tongue?

BEATRICE / TEDDY
Yours, if you talk of tails: And so farewell.

RICHARD / AUSTIN
What, with my tongue in your tail?

(BEATRICE *slaps him.*)

RICHARD / AUSTIN (*cont'd*)
By my sword, Beatrice, thou lovest me!

BEATRICE / TEDDY
I really don't!

RICHARD / AUSTIN
Beatrice, this is all my own doing;
I'm unpracticed in the art of wooing.
The words that I'm saying seem to be wrong –

(PUCK *magically hands* RICHARD *a ukulele.*
Wind chimes.)

RICHARD / AUSTIN
(*getting an idea*) P'rhaps I can sway you by singing a song.
Therefore, since I cannot prove a lover
I'm determined to prove – a vaudevillian!

> (BEATRICE *sighs theatrically.* RICHARD *plays and sings. The chords are notated above each line. The melody can be obtained by e-mailing Josef Weinberger Ltd.*)

RICHARD / AUSTIN (*cont'd*)

F
Sigh no more, lady, sigh no more

C
Men were deceivers ever

F
One foot in sea and one on shore

   G7   *C*
To one thing constant never

F
So sigh not so and let them go

C
And be you blithe and bonny

F
Converting all your sounds of woe

      G7
Into –

> (*He stops singing to tell a joke.*)

> Hey, I was upset when Beatrice said she didn't love me but I slept like a baby. I puked and cried and wet the bed.

> (*He sings again.*)

F
So sigh not so and let them go

C
And be you blithe and bonny

F
Converting all your sounds of woe

        G7
Into –

                    (*He stops again to tell a joke.*)

                    Hey, my shrink said I was crazy. I said I
                    want a second opinion. He said, "Okay,
                    you're a hunchback too."

                    (*He sings again.*)

F
Converting all your sounds of woe

        G7
Into –

                    (*Another joke.*)

                    Hey, they laughed when I said I wanted to
                    be a comedian. Well, they're not laughing
                    now!

                    (*Sings the big finish.*)

F
Converting all your sounds of woe

        G7   C
Into hey nonny nonny!

(*spoken, aside*) Was ever woman in this humor woo'd?
Was ever woman in this humor won?

BEATRICE / TEDDY
(*touched*) That song proved to me you're not such a chump.

RICHARD / AUSTIN
(*innocently*) Does that mean you love me and wanna hump?

(*Offended again, she slaps him and exits.*)

Still got it!

(RICHARD *exits.*)

SCENE NINE: INTERJECTION
(REED, TEDDY)

REED *removes his* PUCK *gear.*

REED   Richard Duke of Gloucester, everybody!
              Now, while Austin is changing, I should
              mention right here that we're going to skip
              ahead to Act Two, Scene One Hundred
              and Thirty-Two, in which Hamlet gives
              his famous advice to the players. But in
              this early work, the players are actually
              characters you may recognize . . .

              (REED *exits.*)

SCENE TEN: ACT TWO, 132
(HAMLET, LADY MACBETH, BOTTOM,
VIOLA, PUCK, RICHARD, ARIEL)

HAMLET *enters.*

HAMLET / AUSTIN
The actors are come hither. I have heard
That guilty creatures sitting at a play

Have by the very cunning of the scene
Been struck to the soul!

> *(Two players enter:* VIOLA, *a woman
> disguised as a man, and* NICK BOTTOM.*)*

VIOLA & BOTTOM
(*singing*) Hey, diddly-dee
An actors life for me –

HAMLET / AUSTIN
Welcome, good friends!

BOTTOM / REED
(*in a silly lower-class accent*) 'Tis I, Nick Bottom the
    weaver, my lord.

VIOLA / TEDDY
And Viola is –

> (BOTTOM *smacks him.*)

Cesario is your servant's name, fair prince.

HAMLET / AUSTIN
Masters, you are all –

BOTTOM / REED   (*interrupting*) The best actors in the world,
                either for tragedy, comedy, history, pastoral,
                pastoral-comical –

VIOLA / TEDDY   Historical-pastoral, tragical-historical –

BOT. / REED   Half-hour sitcom, hour-long drama –

VIOLA / TEDDY   Melodramatical soap operatical –

BOT. / REED   Unscripted reality –

BOTH	Or *Athenians Got Talent.* Thank you.
	(*They bow.* BOTTOM *holds out his hand for coins.*)
BOT. / REED	Yeah? No? Okay.
HAM. / AUSTIN	Yes, well. Friends, we'll hear a play tomorrow –
BOT. / REED	First, good Hamlet prince, say what the play treats on.
	(HAMLET *tries to.*)
	Then read the names of the actors.
	(HAMLET *tries again.*)
	And so grow to a point, doncha know!
HAM. / AUSTIN	Marry! Our play is "The most lamentable comedy and most cruel death of Pyramus and Thisbe."
BOT. / REED	A very good piece of work, I assure you. Name what part I am for, and proceed.
HAM. / AUSTIN	You are set down for Pyramus. A lover that kills himself most gallantly for love.
BOT. / REED	That will ask for some tears in the true performing of it.
HAM. / AUSTIN	Speak the speech, I pray you, as I pronounced it to you –
	(BOTTOM *interrupts* HAMLET, *never letting him finish.*)

BOT. / REED   If I do it, let the audience look to their eyes.
                     I will move storms!

HAM. / AUSTIN   Nor do not saw the air too much with your
                     hand, thus –

BOT. / REED   Oh, let me play a lion, too! I will roar – (*He
                     roars.*)

HAM. / AUSTIN   Suit the action to the word, the word to the
                     action!

BOT. / REED   I could also play Hercules.

HAM. / AUSTIN   You're playing Pyramus!

BOT. / REED   Amateur.

HAM. / AUSTIN   Now you, Cesario, you must take Thisbe on
                     you.

VIOLA / TEDDY   What is Thisbe, a wandering knight?

HAM. / AUSTIN   Thisbe is the lady that Pyramus must love.

VIOLA / TEDDY   Nay, faith, let me not play a woman. I have a
                     beard. Coming.

BOT. / REED   Let me play Frisbee too!

VIOLA / TEDDY   Ay, let us play Frisbee.

                     (*They throw a frisbee.*)

HAM. / AUSTIN
(*aside*) As much as I loathe to appear a jerk,
This play within a play's not gonna work.

                     (*He exits.*)

BOT. / REED
I'll speak in a monstrous little voice –

> (*Alternating high and low voices.*) "Frisbee,
> Frisbee!" "Ah Pyramus, my lover dear!"
> (*Noticing* HAMLET *is gone.*) Hey, where'd
> he go? (*Sees* VIOLA *taking off her hat and
> britches, revealing long hair and a skirt.*)

Viola! What danger will it be to us,
Maid as you are, to travel forth like that!
Put thyself back in poor and mean attire.

> (*He exits.*)

VIOLA / TEDDY
(*putting her hair back under her hat*) Oh Bottom, how
weary are my spirits!
Disguise fair nature with hard-favoured rage.
(*putting her trousers back on*) Once more into the britches,
   dear friends, once more . . .

> (PUCK *enters, unseen.*)

PUCK / REED
Maybe I've been barking up the wrong tree
Richard might want not a she, but a he!
Here's one of a pair of right likely lads:
Let's see if Richard prefers boobs or 'nads!

> (PUCK *gestures and* RICHARD *enters, glowing
> with a terrible case of puppy love.* PUCK
> *sits in the audience as* RICHARD *spies
> "Cesario."*)

RICHARD / AUSTIN
Hello there! What's your name?

VIOLA / TEDDY
Cesario, my lord. A poor player

Who struts and frets his hour upon the stage.

> (*She starts to leave.*)

RICHARD / AUSTIN
I am Richard, Duke of Gloucester.

> (VIOLA *turns back quickly, forgetting she's
> in disguise.*)

VIOLA / TEDDY
A Duke!
(*aside*) I *love* Dukes.

RICHARD / AUSTIN
Dost thou know the lady Beatrice?

VIOLA / TEDDY
I know her not, my lord, but will do my
Best to woo your lady.
                         (*aside*) Oh, this is strife!
Whoe'er I woo, myself would be his wife.

RICHARD / AUSTIN
Come hither, boy.

> (VIOLA *leaps across, getting as close as
> possible to* RICHARD.)

           If ever thou shalt love,
In the sweet pangs of it remember me;
For such as I am, all true lovers are.

> (*Turning and looking closely at "him".*)

My life upon't, young though thou art, thine eye
Hath stay'd upon some favor that it loves.
What kind of woman is't?

VIOLA / TEDDY

                Of your complexion.

RICHARD / AUSTIN
She is not worth thee then. What years, i'faith?

VIOLA / TEDDY
About your years, my lord.

RICHARD / AUSTIN

                Too old, by heaven!

VIOLA / TEDDY
Say that some lady, as perhaps there is,
Hath for your love as great a pang of heart
As you have for Beatrice.

RICHARD / AUSTIN

               No woman's heart's
So big, to hold so much.

VIOLA / TEDDY

             Ay, but I know
Too well what love women to men may owe.

                (*They are nose to nose, about to kiss, but
                they dare not. They break apart, clearing
                their throats and posturing.*)

RICH. / AUSTIN   Football!

VIOLA / TEDDY   Testicles!

RICH. / AUSTIN   Lady bits!

VIOLA / TEDDY   Farting farting fart fart farts!

RICH. / AUSTIN

(*aside*) Oh, I never knew love like this before!

VIOLA / TEDDY
(*aside*) Oh, I'd really like to do that some more!

> (*They exit, in different directions.* PUCK
> *dances with glee.*)

PUCK / REED
Up and down, up and down,
I will lead them up and down!
I send them here, I send them everywhere;
A merrier hour was ne'er wasted there.
I care not if they should die or should live;
A puck is exactly what I don't give.

(ARIEL *enters.*)

ARIEL / TEDDY
Ill-met by moonlight, proud mischievous Puck.

PUCK / REED
What, jealous, Ariel? Fairy, skip hence!

ARIEL / TEDDY
Tarry, rash pixie. Am not I thy foe?

PUCK / REED
Why art thou here? Are there no more Scottish
Ladies you can set upon a Danish prince?

ARIEL / TEDDY
Oh! No more smart women you can strike dumb
With your sad and simple lovestruck hunchback?

PUCK / REED
Your annoying antics do make me mad.

ARIEL / TEDDY
Your mischievous tricks make us all look bad!

I can do whatever I want, for my
Master Prospero hath power and art
Greater than yours and all others combined.

PUCK / REED
My master Oberon is the Fairy King:
Greater than anyone or anything.

ARIEL / TEDDY
We'll see who's the greatest magician of all,
And who will rise up and who'll take the fall.

PUCK / REED
Come, then, if you dare, come and do your worst.
Just remember, you'll have to catch me first!

(PUCK *disappears*.)

ARIEL / TEDDY
Doggone it! He's fast, and now also gone.
So I'm forced to visit King Oberon.

(*She exits*.)

SCENE ELEVEN: INTERJECTION
(AUSTIN)

AUSTIN *enters*.

AUSTIN   Ladies and gentlemen, another thing I
                      love about Shakespeare's first play is that
                      he gives some of his smaller more crowd-
                      pleasing characters larger more prominent
                      roles. So with that in mind, we take you
                      now to Act Three, Scene Five Hundred and
                      Eleven, which takes place in Scotland.

(*He exits*.)

SCENE TWELVE: ACT THREE, 511
(WITCHES, PUCK)

Thunder. 1ST WITCH *enters. She wears a wig and ugly teeth.*

1ST WITCH / TEDDY
When shall we three meet again?
In thunder, lightning, or in rain?

> (2ND WITCH *enters, wearing a wig and half-mask.*)

2ND WITCH / REED
(*cackling*) When the hurly-burly's done,
When the battle's lost and won.

1ST WITCH / TEDDY
Where hast thou been, sister?

2ND WITCH / REED
Killing swine.

1ST WITCH / TEDDY
(*looking at the audience*) I think you missed a few.

> (*They both cackle.* 3RD WITCH *enters. She's a puppet head operated from under a hood, so that the actor's head and arm is the witch's hunchback and neck, a fake arm is stitched to the side, and the actor's other arm is free.*)

3RD WITCH / AUSTIN
(*cackling*) By the pricking of my thumbs,
Something wicked this way comes!

1ST WITCH / TEDDY
Sister, where thou?

3rd Witch / Austin
On the Moors.

2nd Witch / Reed
Stay off the moors!

3rd Witch / Austin
Oh, but I love to be on the Moors,
Especially the Moor of Venice!

(*They cackle hysterically.*)

All Three
The weird sisters, hand in hand,
Posters of the sea and land,
Thus do go, about, about –

1st Witch / Teddy
Thrice to thine –

3rd Witch / Austin
And thrice to mine –

All Three
And thrice again, to make up nine.
Fair is foul and foul is fair,
Hover through the fog and filthy air!

(*They cough.*)

1st Witch / Teddy
My weird sisters two, who both do appear,
You're prob'ly wond'ring why I called you here

2nd Witch / Reed
From Scotland is stolen one of ours,

3rd Witch / Austin
She was whisked away despite our powers.

1ST WITCH / TEDDY
We cannot ignore this kind of attack,

ALL THREE
So Lady Macbeth we have to bring back!
Double, double, toil and trouble,
Fire burn and cauldron bubble.

1ST WITCH / TEDDY
Eye of newt and toe of frog

2ND WITCH / REED
Wool of bat and tongue of dog

3RD WITCH / AUSTIN
Scale of dragon, tooth of rat

1ST WITCH / TEDDY
Baby's finger, Schrodinger's cat

2ND WITCH / REED
Things that are never used, in part:

ALL THREE
Democrat brain, Republican heart!

(*They cackle.*)

1ST WITCH / TEDDY
A charger from the phone you lost

2ND WITCH / REED
Packets at home of fast food sauce

3RD WITCH / AUSTIN
An old device that makes fondue

1st WITCH / TEDDY
A VCR that once was new

2nd WITCH / REED
Public pay phones

3rd WITCH / AUSTIN
Nipples on men

ALL THREE
Superfluous all, we say again.

>   (*During these next two lines,* 2ND WITCH
>   *exits, handing the half-mask off to* TEDDY,
>   *who now plays both parts.*)

ALL THREE
Double, double, toil and trouble,
Fire burn and cauldron bubble.

3RD WITCH / AUSTIN
Cool it with a baboon's blood

1ST WITCH / TEDDY
Then the charm is firm and gud!

3RD WITCH / AUSTIN
Gud?

1ST WITCH / TEDDY
It rhymes with blood.

3RD WITCH / AUSTIN
That doesn't make any sense, you stupid witch . . .

>   (PUCK *appears.*)

PUCK / REED
Secret, black, and midnight hags, wassup witches?

>   (*The witches scream, startled.*)

Have no fear in your hovel so squalid

Relax, I am here to do you a solid.

3RD WITCH / AUSTIN
Wait! What is your name? Art thou Ariel?

PUCK / REED
My name is Puck, Ariel's enemy.
Ariel took Lady Macbeth to help
A melancholy Dane 'scape his torment.

1ST WITCH / TEDDY
Saucy and overbold, how does she dare
To trade and traffic with Lady Macbeth?

PUCK / REED
I too want to punish that sprite, Ariel.
Frankly, she makes my life a living hell.

3RD WITCH / AUSTIN
Many thanks, little pixie, time will tell –

1ST WITCH / 3RD WITCH
If we can revenge on that sprite Ariel!

ALL THREE WITCHES
Away, away!

(*They cackle evilly and exit.*)

SCENE THIRTEEN: INTERJECTION
(REED, AUSTIN, TEDDY)

REED *returns.*

REED   Here's what's coming up. All of
                  Shakespeare's plays reach a climax right
                  in the middle. Think of the closet scene in
                  Hamlet, or the lovers arguing in the woods
                  in *Midsummer*, or the chandelier falling

in Shakespeare's *Phantom of the Opera*. The same thing happens here, when a mighty tempest rips through the entire play, affecting every character we see and most of the ones we don't. And in the middle of this tempest is one single ship that carries every Shakespearean character who ever ended up in Italy.

(AUSTIN *enters with the manuscript.*)

AUSTIN Wait, Reed, I can't bel – (*To the audience.*) I'm sorry. (*To* REED.) I can't believe you've almost completely cut the Cardenio story line. This first play proves that Cardenio *is* one of Shakespeare's plays, and is based on *Don Quixote.*

REED We don't have time and it's got nothing to do with Puck and Ariel.

AUSTIN Ugh. Fine.

(TEDDY *enters as* AUSTIN *exits in a huff.*)

TEDDY Wait, Reed, as long as we're stopped, things are going to get really complicated right before intermission. And we still don't have enough actors to play all the characters.

REED Look, it's going to be fine. I made a bunch more cuts and we should be . . .

AUSTIN (*entering*) Hey! Did you make a bunch more cuts?

REED No!

(AUSTIN *slowly and suspiciously exits.*)

             (*To* TEDDY.) So I made a bunch more cuts and now there are only about twelve characters at the end of Act One.

TEDDY   Yeah, but Austin's still going to have to double up as both Oberon and Prospero. How's that gonna work?

REED   Easy. He just puts on the hat and beard and boom, he's Prospero.

TEDDY   Nobody's gonna buy that.

REED   Are you kidding? They've been buying it all night. You put on that wig and people buy you're a girl. Austin puts on a hat and people buy that he's handsome. It's called the suspension of disbelief!

TEDDY   What?

REED   It's what theatre is all about.

TEDDY   Sure, actors like us know that, but –

REED   Come on, Teddy. Everyone in the world is an actor!

TEDDY   (*re: the audience*) Those are not actors! Those are valuable members of society!

REED   No, they're not. Look at them! They're actors! And they're going to help us out with the tempest at the end of the act. We'll get a big blue cloth, we'll have Dale come up here and hold one end and Gail – that's Gail right there – how ya' doin, Gail? – she'll come up and hold the other end and then we'll . . .

> (*He whispers.* TEDDY *agrees with what he hears but then asks . . .*)

TEDDY   Wait, what about the stern British monarch who is practically perfect in every way?

REED   (*scolding*) No! I cut Mary, Queen of Poppins. Start the scene!

> (*He exits.* TEDDY *starts the next scene.*)

SCENE FOURTEEN: ACT THREE, 740:THE TEMPEST
(ARIEL, OBERON)

ARIEL / TEDDY
How now, Oberon? Dost remember me?

> (OBERON, *the King of the Fairies, enters. Very butch, magical, and impressive looking.*)

OBERON / AUSTIN
Art thou Peaseblossom? Cobweb? Tinkerbell!

ARIEL / TEDDY
Ariel, the pixie sprite, bearing
Such news as would give my lord the shingles.

OBERON / AUSTIN
I'm listening.

ARIEL / TEDDY
It pains me to tell you thy precocious
Puck hath stolen away from Fairyland
And frighted maidens of the villagery,
And relocated two twins to Italy,
And played matchmaker to a hunchbacked Duke
Named Quasimodo.

OBERON / AUSTIN
(*confused*) Be he not a full modo?

ARIEL / TEDDY
Nay. Merely quasi. Actually, I do but jest. His name is
Richard. The point is, Puck attendeth not to his duties.

OBERON / AUSTIN
Why should gentle Puck cross his Oberon?

ARIEL / TEDDY
I know not. But I thought you should know.
Methinks you were wrong choosing him over me.

OBERON / AUSTIN
This is not good.

> (OBERON *gestures and the tempest begins.*
> *Thunder and wind sounds.*)

OBERON / AUSTIN (*cont'd*)
Therefore the winds, piping to us in vain,
As in revenge have sucked up from the sea,
And every pelting river's made so proud
That they have overborn their continents.

ARIEL / TEDDY
(*beginning to have to yell*)
And through this distemperature I can see
The seasons alter: I know not which is which.

OBERON / AUST. I'll take it from here, Tinkerbell.

ARIEL / TEDDY   Ariel!

OBERON / AUST. (*as he goes*) Doesn't matter.

ARIEL / TEDDY   It matters to me!

(*aside*) Gentle Puck, your future I foresee:
In so much trouble you're going to be!

(ARIEL *exits.*)

SCENE FIFTEEN: ACT THREE, 757: THE TEMPEST
(PUCK, WITCHES)

PUCK *enters.*

PUCK / REED
I hear a distant rumbling going on,
Which sounds like the work of King Oberon.
He's angry about something, I can tell,
And I'm sure it's because of Ariel.
She leadeth me like a Puck to the slaughter.
Well, I know how to fight water with water.

(*Calling.*) Where my witches at?

(*He exits. The* WITCHES *enter one by one.*)

ALL THREE WITCHES
Thunder lightning and in rain
When shall we three meet again?
Though thy boat cannot be lost,
Thou shall all be tempest-tossed!

(*They cackle.* 1ST WITCH *exits.*)

2ND WITCH / 3RD WITCH
Blow, blow, yes we can!
If we can't do it, no one can!
Go – witches!!

(*Tempest noise. They cackle and exit.*)

SCENE SIXTEEN: ACT THREE, 773: THE TEMPEST
(POMPEY, CARDENIO, PERICLES)

The tempest rises. POMPEY *enters, dressed like a pirate with a hook for one hand.*

POMPEY / TEDDY
(*sings*) Full fathom five thy father lies;
Of his bones are coral made;
Those are pearls that were his eyes:
Nothing of him that doth fade.
Yo ho yo ho, a Shakespeare pirate me!

> (CARDENIO *enters, swaying as the ship rocks. He wears a conquistador-type helmet.*)

CARD. / REED   Capitan Pompey!

POMP. / TEDDY   Ay, what ist, Cardenio?

CARD. / REED   Can you command these elements to silencio? I come from Navarre to dream the impossible dream.

POMP. / TEDDY   Ar, fear not, lad. We're making a lot of stops in Italy: Padua, Verona, Venice, Messina, Bella Italia, Pizza Express – Greggs – ! [*Localize these restaurants.*] And then we'll arrive on the coast of Bohemia.

CARD. / REED   Does Bohemia have a coast?

POMP. / TEDDY   It does not, but I know a guy who knows a guy.

> (PERICLES *enters, weaving. The ship rocks.*)

PERI. / AUSTIN   Captain! The ship is rocking –

POMP. / CARD.	Then don't come a-knocking!

(*They high-five.* POMPEY'S *hook stabs* CARDENIO'S *hand.*)

CARD. / REED	Ay, ay, ay! Dios mio!
POMP. / TEDDY	Sorry. What is it, Pericles?
PERI. / AUSTIN	My wife is about to give birth down below!
CARD. / REED	Don't all women give birth down below?
POMP. / TEDDY	(*He starts to high-five* REED, *but stops.*) Pound it.

(REED *fist-bumps the hook instead.*)

PERI. / AUSTIN	No, I mean below decks. In our cabin.
POMP. / CARD.	Ohh!

(*The ship rocks. They sway from side to side until* CARDENIO *falls overboard and water splashes on.*)

CARD. / REED	(*off*) El splash!
PERI. / AUSTIN	Oh, no! Cardenio's fallen overboard.

POMP. / TEDDY
Alas, we cannot reverse course to save him. I fear Cardenio's forever lost.
I pray you now, keep below. You do assist the storm.

(PERICLES *exits.*)

There is a tide in the affairs of men! A plague upon this howling!

(*He exits.*)

SCENE SEVENTEEN: ACT THREE, 796: THE TEMPEST
(LEAR, DROMIO)

KING LEAR *enters, old, with a long white beard and an
extremely short cane.*

LEAR / REED
They durst not do it. My three daughters could not, would
not do it. O Fool, I shall go mad!

(*Sees he's alone.*)

Fool? Fool, catch up!

(DROMIO *runs on.*)

DROMIO / TEDDY
Sorry, your majesty! Sorry! I lost you on this blasted heath!
(*aside*) I lost Juliet and ended up here:
I'm now the Fool to an old fool named Lear.

(*Thunder. Tempest noise.*)

DROMIO / TEDDY (*cont'd*)
Wow! So foul and fair a day I haven't seen!

(*More lightning.* DROMIO *screams and exits.*)

LEAR / REED
Blow, winds, and crack your cheeks!

(*Fart noise.*)

Sorry. I'm old.

(*He exits.*)

SCENE EIGHTEEN: ACT THREE, 808: THE TEMPEST
(Ariel, Prospero)

Ariel *enters.*

Ariel / Teddy
All hail, great master, great Prospero, hail!

> (Prospero *enters, the great magician and
> former Duke of Milan. He has a white beard
> and conical hat.*)

Prospero / Austin
Hast thou, spirit, created a tempest
Though I forbade thee?

Ariel / Teddy
Here's my story, I think it will tickle.
I've gotten into a bit of a pickle.

Prospero / Austin
Dost thou forget from what torment I already freed thee?

Ariel / Teddy
I do not, sir! And I come to answer
Thy best pleasure and strong bidding if you'll
Bring thy magic to bear on my behalf.

Prospero / Austin
Fine. Just this once. But only because I really like tempests.

Ariel / Teddy
Thank you, master!

Prospero / Austin
Go make thyself like a nymph of the sea!

(PUCK *runs in with a blue cloth and hands
it to* ARIEL. *They wave it on the ground and
slowly raise it up vertically to represent
the rising tempest. The lights and sounds
change as* PROSPERO *commands.*)

PROSPERO / AUSTIN (*cont'd*)
You elves of hills, brooks, standing lakes, and groves,
And you that on the sands with printless foot
Do chase the ebbing Neptune, I bedim
The noontide sun, and call forth the mutinous
Winds, and twixt the green sea and azur'd vault
Set roaring war!

(PROSPERO *exits.*)

SCENE NINTEEN: ACT THREE, 824: THE TEMPEST
(EVERYONE)

*The tempest noise rises. As they talk, they hold and wave a
blue cloth across the stage. This is the stormy ocean.*

PUCK / REED
If by your art, my dear Ariel, you've
Put the wild waters in this roar, allay them!

(*Pointing.*)

Dale! C'mere!

ARIEL / TEDDY
Methought I saw a thousand fearful wrecks,
Ten thousand men that fishes gnawed upon!

(*Pointing.*)

Hey, Gail! Come up here!

> (*They get* DALE *and* GAIL *to hold the cloth, and pass out squirt guns to the front row of the audience.*)

PUCK / REED
Inestimable stones, unvalued jewels,
All scattered in the bottom of the sea!

ARIEL / TEDDY
O now begins the tempest to my soul!
I pass, methinks, the melancholy flood;
The seaweed is always greener in somebody else's lake!

> (PERICLES *appears behind the blue cloth. The actors struggle to stay afloat behind the blue cloth 'waves', but disappear and change costumes quickly before bobbing up as someone new. If necessary, encourage the audience members with squirt guns to fire away.*)

PERICLES / AUSTIN
(*bobbing up*) Still thy deafening dreadful thunders! My wife!

> (REED *screams as he tosses a baby to* AUSTIN.)

PERICLES / AUSTIN
My baby!

> (*He sinks as* POMPEY *bobs up.*)

POMPEY / TEDDY
The sea is impatient! What cares these roarers that spit their water!

JULIET / AUSTIN
(*bobbing up and admiring Pompey*)
Oh heavenly sight, that I ne'er saw true beauty till this night!

> *(They sink below the waves.* CARDENIO *bobs up.)*

CARDENIO / REED
I'm lost! I'm lost! I now go to the great Greggs in the sky.

> *(He sinks.* TEDDY *bobs up.)*

TEDDY
(singing)
We'll all be deader
Down where it's wetter
Under the sea – !

> *(*AUSTIN *reaches up, grabs* TEDDY'S *clamshell, and pulls him down.)*

LEAR / REED
(bobbing up) Rumble thy bellyful! Spit, fire! Spout, rain –
  oh, good spouting!

> *(He screams and sinks.)*

HAMLET / AUSTIN
(bobbing up) To drown or not to drown, that is the question!

> *(He sinks.)*

BOTTOM / REED
(bobbing up) Look at my acting – I'm moving storms, don't
  ya know!

> *(He screams and sinks.)*

PROSPERO / AUSTIN
(bobbing up, waving his staff) Drench the steeples! Drown
  the cocks!

> *(He sinks.)*

TEDDY
(singing) Oh brave new world –

> (AUSTIN *pulls him down by the clamshell.*)

Hey! Hands off the boob!

LADY MACBETH / REED
(*bobbing up*) Is this a lifeboat I see before me?

> (*She screams and sinks.*)

RICHARD / AUSTIN
(*bobbing up*) A boat! A boat! My kingdom for a boat!

> (*He sinks.*)

TEDDY
(*singing*) Can you feel the storm tonight –

> (AUSTIN *and* REED *stand up with larger
> squirt cannons. They squirt* TEDDY*, then
> point their guns at the audience.*)

AUSTIN
You're just lucky they told us not to shoot you.

> (*He and* REED *look at each other*)

Oh, screw it.

> (*They squirt the audience.* AUSTIN *gathers
> costumes and props and exits as* PUCK
> *and* ARIEL *gather the cloth and send the
> volunteers back to their seats. As they do . . .*)

REED
Dale and Gail, everybody!

ARIEL / TEDDY
I brought on this tempest, Puck. Do you yield?

PUCK / REED
Never! 'Tis *my* tempest dampens this field!

ARIEL / TEDDY
I'll prove the finest fairy magician –

PUCK / REED
Not before first I call –

BOTH
                    – Intermission!

                    (*They exit, glaring at each other as they go.*
                    Blackout. End of Act One.)

ACT TWO

SCENE TWENTY: ACT FOUR, PROLOGUE
(CHORUS)

REED and TEDDY enter formally. They play a familiar melody on kazoos. The cloaked hooded figure – CHORUS – appears again, moving powerfully. But he recognizes the music and throws back his hood, shaking his head and gesturing to the others to stop. They do.

Then CHORUS turns front, realizes the house lights are still up, and brings them down magically using his arms. Then he brings them up again. Then down, then up and down until he stops.

Then, just before the other two begin to blow again, CHORUS brings down the lights on TEDDY.

TEDDY   Hey!

               (REED *laughs and* CHORUS *brings the lights down on him, too.*)

REED   Hey . . .

               (CHORUS *acquiesces and gestures for the two to begin. They move center into the remaining light, raise their kazoos and begin to blow. A magnificent recorded trumpet fanfare sounds. They finish with a flourish and exit with great dignity.*)

CHORUS / AUSTIN
I come no more to make you laugh; things now
That bear a weighty and serious brow
We now present. I hope you all have peed.
Now, in the name of Time I have a need
To tell you things have changed. I turn my glass
And so many hours and days do pass

That it's not clear exactly when we are.
So too I spin my globe to bring the far-
Off lands together in this one forum,
Where love is lost and so's all decorum.
Think and you shall then be surprised to see
The very persons of our noble story
Are transformed: Both the evils and the goods
Are thrown together in these self-same woods.
Though in the past you once did see them great,
And with such power and direction of late
They were much blessed; now, in a moment, see
How soon this mightiness meets misery.
What was silly and slightly mysterious
Now is mortal and mighty serious.
And all because, as you remember well,
The merry war twixt Puck and Ariel.
Gentle spectators, let us continue
And see what endurance is still left in you.

(*He bows.*)

SCENE TWENTY ONE: WELCOME BACK!
(AUSTIN, REED, TEDDY)

REED *and* TEDDY *enter and join* AUSTIN, *who once again ditches his cloak.*

REED	Welcome back, everybody!
TEDDY	Make sure you've turned off your cell phones.
AUSTIN	I hope you drank plenty of coffee because we still have forty hours to go.
REED	Minutes! We've still got forty minutes to go!
AUSTIN	Right! Minutes. Sorry.

REED   That's right. We're performing here through
                        (*closing date*) so if you enjoy the show,
                        please tell all your friends on Facebook. If
                        you don't enjoy the show, please tell all your
                        friends on MySpace. Now – we begin the
                        second half of the show with Shakespeare's
                        Act Four, in which the tempest that ended
                        the first half has washed ashore all one
                        thousand six hundred and thirty-nine of
                        Shakespeare's characters on a wooded
                        island.

TEDDY   Among those now lost in this forest are
                        a merchant from Venice, a Danish prince
                        picked up from an English vessel, the entire
                        court of the King of Naples, seventeen
                        different pairs of twins, and an Egyptian
                        queen. You should see the asp on her.

AUSTIN   You should also know that Richard Duke of
                        Gloucester has been crowned King Richard
                        the Third –

REED   A soldier named Titus Andronicus is
                        surviving in the woods by eating pies made
                        out of his enemies –

TEDDY   A young poet named Orlando is designing
                        theme parks –

AUSTIN   Yes he is. The little wooden puppet
                        Petruchio has been swallowed by a giant
                        whale –

REED   Falstaff is still on the run with Dromio's
                        gold –

TEDDY   Dromio is still on the run from Juliet –

AUSTIN   Skulking and scheming in the woods is the
               evil bitter Puritan lieutenant Malvoliago –

REED   And Sir Thomas More and Merlin are
               wandering around looking for better plays to
               be in.

TEDDY   Wait, Merlin?

REED   Yes, Shakespeare's first play proves that
               he did indeed write the disputed work *The
               Birth of Merlin.*

TEDDY   *Sword in the Stone!*

BOTH   Disney! Whoah!

               (TEDDY *and* REED *make a "mind blown"
               gesture and exit.*)

AUSTIN   Son of a – . Anyway, ladies and gentlemen,
               we take you now deep into the mysterious
               Forest of Ardenbirnam, where Puck and
               Ariel are trying to undo the mess they've
               created.

               (AUSTIN *exits as* –)

SCENE TWENTY TWO: ACT FOUR, 825: THE WOODS
                    (PUCK, ARIEL)

PUCK *and* ARIEL *run in.*

PUCK / REED
See what thou hast done?

ARIEL / TEDDY
                See what *thou* hast done?

PUCK / REED
Thou tricked my master Oberon into
Calling up a storm that changed the seasons.

ARIEL / TEDDY
I'm sure the Fairy King had his reasons.
Those were but wild and whirling winds you and
The weird witches whipped up! 'Tis *thy* negligence!

PUCK / REED
Thou liest, unfair fairy. I merely
Called your bluff.

ARIEL / TEDDY
       And hast thou, pixie, had enough?
The tempest hath blown away each border –

PUCK / REED
And any such resemblance of order.
(*aside*) As 'tis, Oberon will be mad indeed.

ARIEL / TEDDY
(*aside*) And I by Prospero shall not be freed.

PUCK / REED
All that was torn apart by the weather –

ARIEL / TEDDY
We have to somehow put back together.

PUCK / REED
Everything can be fixed, on the double –

BOTH
(*aside*) And I can still get him/her in more trouble.

PUCK / REED
(*aside*) With good fortune –

ARIEL / TEDDY
(*aside*)
       With a wee bit of luck –

PUCK / REED
(*aside*) I'll out-fairy Ariel.

ARIEL / TEDDY
(*aside*)
       I'll out-Puck Puck!

PUCK / REED
(*aside*) And all will be fixed –

ARIEL / TEDDY
(*aside*)
       And all will now heal –

BOTH
(*aside*) And he/she'll never know how truly I feel.

          (*On that note of uncertainty,* PUCK *exits.*)

SCENE TWENTY THREE: ACT FOUR, 826
(PUCK, BOTTOM, ARIEL, CLEOPATRA, REED, TEDDY,
AUSTIN, FALSTAFF, OBERON, RICHARD, HAMLET)

ARIEL *remains on from the previous scene.*

ARIEL / TEDDY
Oh, Puck. Though you feel you're double my worth,
I too can put a girdle round the earth
And place royalty into my power
With the aid of enchanting Cupid's flower.
Since you brought here Denmark's prince for a while
I'll bring Cleopatra, Queen of the Nile.

          (CLEOPATRA *enters. Strong, imperious, and
          at the moment totally bewitched.*)

ARIEL / TEDDY
Your highness, in this setting botanical,
I give you, for love, this rude mechanical.

> (*She gestures and* BOTTOM *enters doing a tongue-twister warm-up.*)

BOTTOM / REED   Peter Piper picked a peck of pickled
peppers. I'm a mother pheasant plucker,
I pluck mother pheasants, I'm the most
pleasant mother f – oh, gosh! That could go
terribly wrong.

CLEOPATRA / AUSTIN
(*enchanted*) Oh, I do love thee. Therefore go with me.
And I shall fetch thee jewels from the deep
And sing while thou on pressèd flowers sleep.

> (BOTTOM *looks around.*)

BOTTOM / REED
I'm sorry, missus, are you talking to me?

CLEOPATRA / AUSTIN
Let me wait upon thee, lead thee to my chamber.

BOTTOM / REED
Let me – see a man about a horse.

> (*He exits.*)

CLEOPATRA / AUSTIN
(*fighting the enchantment*) I'm no more but a woman, and
   commanded
By such poor passion as the maid that milks
And does the meanest chores.

> (PUCK *enters and freezes* CLEOPATRA.)

PUCK / REED
What hempen homespun have we swaggering here

So near the cradle of the Egypt Queen?
If Ariel thinks a Queen of such class
Can love an ass, then *let's make him an ass!*

(PUCK *exits and* CLEOPATRA *unfreezes.*)

CLEOPATRA / AUSTIN
Oh my lord, my lord,
I will not be triumphed over!

(BOTTOM *starts singing offstage and enters
wearing an ass's head.*)

BOTTOM / REED (*off*)
O Mistress mine, where are you roaming
O stay and hear your true love's coming

(*Enters.*) I can sing both high and low – *hee-haw!*

CLEOPATRA / AUSTIN
(*instantly smitten*) I pray thee gentle Eeyore, sing again.

BOTTOM / REED
(*unconvinced of her sincerity*) I see your flattery. This is to
make an ass of me, eh?

(*She cirles him, examining him closely.*)

CLEOPATRA / AUSTIN
Mine ear is much enamored of thy note.
So is mine eye enthrallèd to thy shape,
And thy fair virtue's force perforce doth move me
On the first view to say, to swear, I love thee.

BOTTOM / REED
Methinks, mistress, you should have little reason for that.
And yet, reason and love keep little company nowadays.

CLEOPATRA / AUSTIN
Thou art as wise as thou art beautiful!

Bottom / Reed
Oh, my stars. Not so neither, but if I had wit enough to get
out of this Hundred Acre Wood –

Cleopatra / Austin
Out of this Hundred Acre Wood do not desire to go.
Thou shalt remain here whether thou wilt or no.
I'm Egypt's queen. In my salad days when
I was green in judgement, I loved Caesar.

Bottom / Reed
(*aside*) Try to keep up with us if you can, folks.
Oh my mistress, age cannot wither you
Nor custom stale your infinite variet – *tee-haw!*

(Ariel *enters and sees her plan has failed.*)

Cleopatra / Austin
Oh, I have immoral longings in me.
I have a love that's something celestial
And oh-so slightly beautifully bestial.

(*They rub noses.*)

Ariel / Teddy
Oh no! Now look at what Puck's gone and done.
He's managed to ruin all of my fun.
I'll have to think of a plan to surpass –

Cleopatra / Austin
It's so true: Everyone loves a nice ass.

Bottom / Reed
Write that down! Forget not that I'm an ass.

(*They start to get busy.*)

Ariel / Teddy
Woah! Shall we their fond pageant see?
Get thee away!

(*Magics them away.*)

Puck has foiled my plan,
And made Cleo love the ass not the man.
Into Oberon will I shift my shape
And command, on pretext of assistance,
That by magic Puck remove Richard's hump.
And the consequence he will not foresee;
A very pox on Puck is what I'll be.

(*Wind chimes.*)

But soft! He comes! And now I must hide!

> (PUCK *enters.* ARIEL *freezes with one hand
> over her face and her arm outstretched like
> a tree branch.*)

PUCK / REED
Cleopatra and Bottom: That was fun
Still, complete satisfaction found I none.
There must be a way I might further prove
My magic stronger than Ariel's groove.
(*Running past Ariel's armpit.*)
Odor most foul! Who is here?
Do not think you cause me fear.

> (ARIEL *remains "invisible" but speaks to*
> PUCK.)

ARIEL / TEDDY
Don't be spooked, Puck –

> (*She clears her throat and now mouths
> the lines as* AUSTIN *speaks them from
> backstage.*)

OBERON / AUSTIN (*off, as* TEDDY *mouths this . . .*)
Don't be spooked, Puck. It's just me.

PUCK / REED
Oberon?

OBERON / AUSTIN (*off, as* TEDDY *mouths this . . .*)
       Yes!

PUCK / REED
         Let me see.

OBERON / AUSTIN (*off, as* TEDDY *mouths this . . .*)
All right, dear Puck.

        (ARIEL *steps into one doorway and* OBERON
        pops out the other. OBERON *is slightly stiff*
        and awkward, as he's actually ARIEL, *and*
        mouths the first line as TEDDY *says it off.*)

ARIEL / TEDDY (*off*)
         I am here.

        (OBERON *clears his throat and speaks in his*
        own voice.)

OBERON / AUSTIN
(*clearing throat*) I am here.

PUCK / REED
        My master!

OBERON / AUSTIN
Fetch you Richard, the duke thou showed me once.
Thou shalt with magic then remove his hump
And he to maids will be Cumberbatch-like. [*Or another
famously handsome man.*]
Adieu, adieu! Remember me!

        (OBERON *walks lamely off and* ARIEL *quickly*
        reappears in the other door, still invisible.)

PUCK / REED
                              'Tis gone.
Oh, happy sprite! All will be right!
True delight when I sight
That Richard's looking swell!
Jack shall have Jill; And naught shall go ill!

> (PUCK *gestures and* RICHARD *enters.*)

PUCK / REED
(*conjuring*) Let yourself be no longer diminished!
Remove that hump: Stand tall and be finished!

> (PUCK *gestures.* RICHARD's *hump disappears
> and his spine straightens.* RICHARD *no
> longer limps.*)

PUCK / REED
With one small part gone; thus, have I reckoned,
Richard the Third is now Richard the Second.

> (REED *exits.*)

RICHARD / AUSTIN
I am amazed – of comfort let me speak.
I have been de-humped; I'm in pain no more.

> (ARIEL *enters.*)

RICHARD / AUSTIN
For God's sake let us stand upon the stage
And tell glad stories of the love of kings!
For I have been mistaken all this while.
It's men I love –

> (ARIEL *gestures and* FALSTAFF *enters, now
> played by* REED.)

RICHARD / AUSTIN
– like you, Sir John.

FALSTAFF / REED
Do I love men? Well, I do love sack!
Would you care to be RE-humped, my lord . . . ?

RICHARD / AUSTIN
Let us make the beast with two backs – !

> (*They run off together, laughing.* ARIEL *is
> delighted.*)

ARIEL / TEDDY
Methinks Puck will now be taken aback:
Jack shall have Jill? No, Jack shall have Jack.

> (*She exits.*)

SCENE 24: ACT IV, 1,562: THE WOODS
(DROMIO, LEAR, WITCHES)

KING LEAR *enters.*

LEAR / REED
Oh, it is not too late. I can still salvage my situation by
giving my three daughters another chance to declare their
love for me!

> (*The* THREE WITCHES *enter,* TEDDY *again
> playing both the* 1ST *and* 2ND WITCHES.)

ALL THREE
Daddy!!

LEAR / REED
                    'Tis still our intent
To shake all cares and business from our age,
Conferring them on younger strengths while we
Unburden'd crawl toward death.

2ND WITCH / 3RD WITCH
Death? No!

3RD WITCH / AUSTIN
You look great!

2ND WITCH / TEDDY
You'll live forever!

3RD WITCH / AUSTIN
Have you lost weight?

LEAR / REED
Silence! Now, know that we have divided
In three our kingdom. Tell me, my daughters,
Which of you shall we say doth love us most?
Our eldest-born, Gonohrrea, speak first.

3RD WITCH / AUSTIN
No! My name's Sycorax!

LEAR / REED
Syphillis?

3RD WITCH / AUSTIN
No, Sycorax! I hate Gonorrhea!

LEAR / REED
So do I. It was your mother's idea
To name you that. I wanted Perfidia.

3RD WITCH / AUSTIN
(*re:* 1ST WITCH) Is that why you named her Chlamydia?

1ST WITCH / TEDDY
Hey! It's Cordelia! Leave me out of it.

LEAR / REED
What says our second daughter, Genital Warts?

2ND WITCH / TEDDY
I profess myself an enemy to
All other joys which the most precious sense

Possesses, and I find I am alone
Felicitate in your dear highness' love.

LEAR / REED
I've no idea what that means.
(*To* 1ST WITCH.) Now, our joy,
What can you say that is more opulent
Than your sisters?

1ST WITCH / TEDDY
Nothing, my lord.

LEAR / REED
Nothing will come from nothing!
How sharper than a serpent's tooth it is
To have a thankless child! Hence, and avoid
My sight, ungrateful witches!

(*They don't move.*)

No? Okay, I'll go then.

(*He exits.*)

1ST WITCH / TEDDY
We've hurt daddy's feelings. What shall we do?

3RD WITCH / AUSTIN
Witch, please. We'll do whatever we have to.

1ST WITCH / 3RD WITCH
(*chanting*) Dogs that bark and cats that mew
We'll get Lady Macbeth and Hamlet too
Expecto Patronum and Allakazoo

3RD WITCH / AUSTIN
We'll get her, my pretties –

1ST WITCH / TEDDY
And her little dog too!

(They cackle and exit.)

SCENE TWENTY FIVE: CALIBAN INTERJECTION
(REED, TEDDY)

REED   Now, I've cut several significant subplots
                        here, including a trip back to the Boar's
                        Head Tavern where we would have met
                        an unfortunate love interest of Mistress
                        Quickly named Sir Premature. So now
                        we move ahead to Act Four, Scene Two
                        Thousand and Seventy-Nine, where the cruel
                        witch, Sycorax, meets her long lost son, the
                        half-man, half-fish, Caliban.

                        (TEDDY *enters wearing a headpiece that
                        looks like something worn by members of
                        the Taliban.*)

CALIBAN / TEDDY
Be not afeared; the isle is full of noises,
Sounds, and sweet airs, that give delight and hurt not.

REED   Wait, wait, wait! Who are you playing?

CALIBAN / TED.   Taliban.

REED   Taliban with a T?

CALIBAN / TED.   Yeah.

REED   It's *Caliban* with a C.

CALIBAN / TED.   Oh crap.

REED   Take that thing off your head. Forget about
                        Caliban. Change into Dromio.

CALIBAN / TED.   Who's playing Princess Isis?

REED   Get out of here!

                (*They exit.*)

SCENE TWENTY SIX: ACT FOUR, 2079: THE WOODS
(JULIET, DROMIO, LEAR, PUCK, BEATRICE, KATE, BEAR)

JULIET *enters.*

JULIET / AUSTIN
My Dromio gone and that is not good!
And now I find myself lost in this wood.

                (DROMIO *enters.*)

DROMIO / TEDDY
Have you seen my brother? He looks like this!

                (*He holds up a large side of a milk carton
                with a hole in it, through which we see
                his face. Above and below the hole it says
                "MISSING! 1-800-THE-BARD".*)

JULIET / AUSTIN
Ugh! His face is far too ugly to see!

                (DROMIO *drops the frame.*)

But yours, good sir, looks very good to me.

DROMIO / TEDDY
Juliet? Oh, not again!

                (DROMIO *screams and exits.*)

JULIET / AUSTIN
Oh dear me, it's like I'm under a spell
I'm one who's loved not wisely *nor* too well.

(PUCK *enters and freezes* JULIET.)

PUCK
Oh, this poor woman, this poor lovelorn dame.
Her love's a curse and my spell is to blame.
But here's a way her problem I can soothe –
The course of true love never did run smooth.

> (PUCK *gestures magically.* BEATRICE *enters,
> not knowing where she is.* PUCK *exits.*)

JULIET / AUSTIN
Oh, this is the very ecstasy of – !

> (*Realizing she's a woman.*)

Oh. Sweet lady, I know not from whence you came.

BEATRICE / TEDDY
From Messina. Beatrice is my name.

JULIET / AUSTIN
(*distracted by a guy in the audience*) What, is't a spirit?
Lord, how it looks about!

> (*Seeing 'Dale'.*)

Dale! I might call Dale a thing divine, for nothing
Natural I ever saw so noble.

> (*She starts to chase him but* BEATRICE *holds
> her back.*)

BEATRICE / TEDDY
Okay, slow down. You can't just fall instantly in love with
every man you see. Especially Dale.

JULIET / AUSTIN
Whoever loved that loved not at first sight?
They do not love that do not show their love.

BEATRICE / TEDDY
Oh, they love least that let men know their love!
I'd rather hear my dog bark at a crow than a man swear he
   love me.

JULIET / AUSTIN
How can you say that?

BEATRICE / TEDDY
Do you not know I am a woman? When I think, I must speak.

> (KATE *enters, still recovering from the
> tempest and relieved to find others.*)

KATE / REED
Ah, there be more women in these strange woods
Wherein that stranger tempest hath left me.

JULIET / AUSTIN
I am Juliet from Verona –

> (BEATRICE *shoves* JULIET *out of the way. She
> is instantly smitten with* KATE.)

BEATRICE / TEDDY
And I – am Beatrice from Messina.

KATE / REED
(*also smitten*) They call me Katherine that do talk of me
In Padua. I'm also called plain Kate,
Bonny Kate, and sometimes Kate Winslet.

JULIET / AUSTIN
(*stepping between them*) My spirits, as in a dream, are all
   bound up.
I have no ambition to see a goodlier man!
I must find a potion. I'll drink it and die!

> (*She starts to go, but they stop her.*)

BEATRICE / KATE
Woah, woah, woah!

BEATRICE / TEDDY
(*to* KATE) What Juliet knows about men isn't much.
Methinks the girl could use a woman's touch.

JULIET / AUSTIN
I see gentlemen are not in your books.

BEATRICE / TEDDY
No, and if they were I'd burn my study.

KATE / REED
I am ashamed that women are so simple
To offer peace when they should stand for war.
Or seek submission and throw power away
When they should be bound to make men obey.

BEATRICE / TEDDY
Don't give thy hand unto a mad-brain ruffian
Who woos in haste and means to wed at leisure.

JULIET / AUSTIN
But what a piece of work is a man! How noble in –

BEATRICE / KATE
No no no no!

KATE / REED
I can never see men but I'm heart-burned an hour after.

BEATRICE / TEDDY
You must learn to swear off men.

KATE / REED
Come sister, let us away.

JULIET / AUSTIN
O thou well-skill'd in curses, stay awhile,
And teach me how to curse all gentlemen!

BEATRICE / TEDDY
Ah, 'tis most easy. First choose an adjective –

KATE / REED
Followed by a compound-worded descriptor –

BEATRICE / TEDDY
And end it with a nasty noun.

> (*For each insult, they point to members of the audience.*)

KATE / REED
For instance: Thou jarring ill-tempered hypocrite!

BEATRICE / TEDDY
Or: Thou inexcrable bald-pated fleshmonger!

KATE / REED
Now you try.

JULIET / AUSTIN
(*reluctantly, but getting more into it as she goes*) Thou slimy
  ugly-looking harpy!

KATE / REED
Hmm . . .

BEATRICE / TEDDY
Not – terrible, but –

KATE / REED
It needs more oomph.

JULIET / AUSTIN
Thou moist phlegm-filled maggot!

KATE / REED
Better!

JULIET / AUSTIN
Thou fugly, fen-sucked scum!

BEATRICE / TEDDY
Nice!

JULIET / AUSTIN
Thou absorbent yellow-porous sponge!

KATE / REED
Ay-ay, Juliet!

JULIET / AUSTIN
Thou sanctimonious, right-winged Farage! [*Or another locally loathed politician.*]

> (KATE *and* BEATRICE *clap in admiration.*)

Politician!

BEATRICE / TEDDY
Girl, you are a woman now.

JULIET / AUSTIN
Critic!

KATE / REED
Two thumbs up!

JULIET / AUSTIN
Lawyer!

KATE / REED
First thing we do –

BEATRICE / KATE
– kill all the lawyers.

JULIET / AUSTIN
Thank you, thou malodorous, mouldy-dripping, merkins!

BEATRICE / TEDDY
That's enough.

JULIET / AUSTIN
Sorry.

KATE / REED
I think our work here is done.

BEATRICE / TEDDY
Not so fast. I have something to announce.
Friends, women, countrymen, lend me your ears:
I come to marry Kate, not to seize her!

KATE / REED
Why, there's a wench!
(*To* JULIET.) Best of luck in these woods!

BEATRICE / TEDDY
(*as they exit*) Come on and kiss me, Kate!

JULIET / AUSTIN
(*delighted*) They taught me their language, and my profit
Is I now know how to curse. Thus, I swear
Not to chase after men. That is my vow –

(REED *in a Bear costume enters, growling.*)

JULIET / AUSTIN
But I can't swear who I'll chase after now! Gimme, gimme,
gimme – !

(*Exit* BEAR, *pursued by* JULIET.)

SCENE TWENTY SEVEN: INTERJECTION
(AUSTIN, REED)

AUSTIN *re-enters immediately, still in his* JULIET *outfit and
carrying the manuscript. He takes his wig off.*

AUSTIN   I wish you could see Shakespeare's stage
                  direction here. It actually says "Exit Bear,
                  pursued by Juliet."

                  (REED *enters, still wearing the bear costume.*)

REED   Austin, we don't have time –

AUSTIN   (*cutting him off*) *This is interesting!!*

                  (*The* BEAR *growls then gives him an "Up
                  yours!" gesture and exits.* AUSTIN *places
                  the manuscript somewhere he can pick it
                  up easily later, or hands it to an audience
                  member if one is close enough.*)

AUSTIN   Ladies and gentlemen, please join me now in
                  booing that evil bitter Puritan lieutenant –
                  Malvoliago!

                  (*He leads the booing as he exits.*)

SCENE TWENTY EIGHT: ACT FOUR, 2183: THE WOODS
(MALVOLIAGO, JULIET, PETRUCHIO,
2ND WITCH, 3RD WITCH)

MALVOLIAGO *enters wearing a long black puritanical robe
with a long black wig. He responds to the audience's boos.*

MALVOLIAGO / TEDDY
I hate you more. And the impure and weak.
And thus it's ultimate power I seek.
If I can get rid of all who lack grace
I will make the world a more Christian place.

                  (JULIET *enters, still mostly under her spell.*)

JULIET / AUSTIN
Hast thou seen a bear? I've lost him again.

(*Noticing him.*)

Ooh, like coffee, I like dark and hot men. Hello, Severus.

MALVOLIAGO / TEDDY
My mistress, are you mad? Is there no respect of place or persons in you?

JULIET / AUSTIN
Thou traitorous stuck-up malmsey-butt!

MALVOLIAGO / TEDDY
How *dare* you!

JULIET / AUSTIN
Thou cancerous ooze-dripping bull's pizzle!

MALVOLIAGO / TEDDY
Off with you, woman!

JULIET / AUSTIN
(*stuck for a third; desperately*) Poopy-head!

(*She exits.* PETRUCHIO *enters.*)

PETRUCHIO / REED
(*high-pitched voice*) Aha!

MALVOLIAGO / TEDDY
Who the devil are *you?*

PETRUCHIO / REED
(*high-pitched voice*) I escaped from the whale's belly and have been turned into a real live boy! I'm Petruchio!

(*singing*) I got no strings, duh-dum-dum-duh
I'm off to wive it wealthily in Padua!

(*spoken*) Buh-bye!

> (*He exits.*)

MALVOLIAGO / TEDDY
If this were play'd upon a stage now, I could condemn it as
an improbable fiction.

3RD WITCH / AUSTIN
(*entering*) By the pricking of my thumbs –

(*noticing* MALVOLIAGO) Something Slytherin this way comes.
  How now, Malvoliago?

> (*The* 2ND WITCH *enters.*)

MALVOLIAGO / TEDDY
Stay, ye imperfect speakers! In this bower,
Can you help me achieve ultimate power?
But first, I'm a Puritan. Is it true?
I must know: You're not lovers, are you?

2ND WITCH / REED
We're the *Weird* Sisters, not the *Queer* Sisters.

3rd WITCH / AUSTIN
Well, except for that one time in college.

> (*They cackle.*)

MALVOLIAGO / TEDDY
Then I'll take your help, because even though
Your evil lifestyle completely astounds,
My total hypocrisy knows no bounds.

2ND WITCH / REED
Just a second –

> (*The* TWO WITCHES *confer, throwing
> judgemental looks at* MALVOLIAGO.)

2ND WITCH / REED
All right. We've decided. We'll do it, no fuss.

3RD WITCH / AUSTIN
But! You will have to do something for us!

(REED *offers him an Elizabethan pistol.*)

2ND WITCH / REED
With this ancient pistol, it would be great
If you could kill a fairy that we hate.

MALVOLIAGO / TEDDY
(*considering*) So it would be a little tit-for-tat?

3RD WITCH / AUSTIN
We'd do it ourselves, but there's no fun in that.

MALVOLIAGO / TEDDY
How will I spot the source of your grief?

3RD WITCH / AUSTIN
(*holding up the handkerchief they describe*)
Easy! She'll carry a white handkerchief.

2ND WITCH
With strawberries on't. It's easy to spot!

MALVOLIAGO / TEDDY
(*taking the pistol*) All right! 'Tis an honest deal that we've got.

2ND WITCH / REED
Excellent! You do your mortal race credit.

3RD WITCH / AUSTIN
We promise you won't live to regret it.

(*They cackle.* MALVOLIAGO *exits.*)

2ND WITCH / REED
Because he'll probably die, right . . . ?

3RD WITCH / AUSTIN
Right!

> (*They cackle as the* 3RD WITCH *exits.*)

2ND WITCH / REED
Yes, yes, yes, there's always a catch.

> (*She exits too.*)

SCENE TWENTY NINE: ACT FOUR, 2207
(ARIEL, RICHARD, VIOLA)

ARIEL *enters.*

ARIEL / TEDDY
Though that was fun and we had a good laugh,
Poor Richard cannot end up with Falstaff.
This ongoing war between Puck and I
Needs to stop soon before one of us dies!

(*gesturing* RICHARD *in; conjuring*)
Since Puck can't succeed with this new attack,
I am now going to put your hunch back.
Though it's a shame to go back on Puck's word,
You must resume being Richard the Third.

> (RICHARD *shrinks back to his hunchback
> state.* ARIEL *exits.*)

RICHARD / AUSTIN
That was indeed strange. 'Twas like a weird dream
In which a man quite different I did seem.
With other men I've been out and about
And frankly my dear, it's freaking me out.

> (VIOLA *enters dressed as* CESARIO *and bows.*)

VIOLA / TEDDY
My lord, I have a confession to make.

Richard / Austin
What is't, my dashing and handsome young rake?

Viola / Teddy
I've deceived you, my lord. My tale's unconventional.

Richard / Austin
I'm sure your deception wasn't intentional.

Viola / Teddy
(*taking hat off and letting hair fall*) I am a woman! I hope
   I'm believed.

Richard / Austin
I'm Richard the Third, and I'm so relieved!
I love you more than one can love another.

Viola / Teddy
I love you much more than a child loves its mother.

Richard / Austin
I'm not the prettiest man you could find.

Viola / Teddy
Love looks not with the eyes but with the mind.

Richard / Austin
And listen to how much we're speaking in rhyme!

Viola / Teddy
It's like we are doing it all of the time!

Richard / Austin
You in your dress –

Viola / Teddy
– and you in your doublet,

Both
We are history's first Rhyming Couplet!

(*They exit, arm in arm.*)

SCENE THIRTY: ACT FOUR, 2225
(FALSTAFF, HENRY V, ARIEL, PUCK)

PUCK *enters.*

PUCK / REED
I feel for Falstaff and all that's occurred:
Toyed with, rejected by Richard the Third.
It's my fault he's in this kind of a scrape;

(ARIEL *enters to overhear this.*)

I'll point him to Pompey to make his escape.
Then I can say I've adhered to my oath.
Puck protects fools and drunks, and Falstaff's both.

(*He gestures.* FALSTAFF *enters, and* PUCK
exits.)

FALSTAFF / AUSTIN
Have I lived to be tossed away by Richard like a barrow of
butcher's offal and thrown in the Thames? You may know by
my size I have a kind of alacrity in sinking.

(ARIEL *freezes* FALSTAFF.)

ARIEL / TEDDY
It's not that easy; in fact, it's a curse.
Puck tries to fix things? Well, I'll make it worse.
(*Conjuring.*) Rebellious dead, rise up in this wood!
Graves at my command have waked their sleepers, op'd, and
   let 'em forth
By my so potent art!

(*She exits.* FALSTAFF *unfreezes. There are
ghostly whispers, wind, and a knocking
indeed.*)

FALSTAFF / AUSTIN
Here's a knocking indeed! Knock, knock! Who's there!

(HENRY V *enters*.)

HENRY V / REED
(*ghostly*) Sir John Falstaff!

FALSTAFF / AUSTIN
No, I'm not Sir John. I'm Sir – Toby Belch!

HENRY V / REED
Peace, ye fat-kidney'd rascal! You lie, i'faith!

FALSTAFF / AUSTIN
Prince Hal! What time of day is it, lad?

HENRY V / REED
Your day of reckoning, Sir John. Prince Hal
No more, I'm King Henry, fifth of that name.
Presume not that I am the thing I was.
Know ye that I am now dead, and that you
Will be visited by three ghosts tonight.
Mark me!

(HENRY V *exits*.)

FALSTAFF / AUSTIN
Mercy, my lord! I do believe in spooks! I do, I do, I *do*
believe in spooks!

(HENRY IV *enters*.)

HENRY IV / TEDDY
So shaken as we are, so wan with care,
Thou art a traitor and a miscreant,
Too good to be so, and too bad to live!

FALSTAFF / AUSTIN
Thou art my Prince Hal's father, Henry Four!

HENRY IV / TEDDY
Ay, I have been dead these many years more.

FALSTAFF / AUSTIN
Marry, my lord, where be these woods?

HENRY IV / TEDDY
This land of such dead souls, this dear dear land,
This royal throne of kings, this sceptred isle,
This poor Britannia, I'm sure she regrets it
It's clear she screwed up by voting for Brexit, [*Localise this couplet.*]
This blessed plot, this earth, this realm, this Great Britain.
Oooh! [*And if you're not performing in Great Britain, localise this as well.*]

                    (*He exits.*)

FALSTAFF / AUSTIN
Oh no! Now I needs must fear the Ghost of Henrys Future!

                (HENRY VIII *enters.*)

HENRY VIII / REED
(*singing*) I'm Henry the Eighth, I am,
Henry the Eighth, I am, I am!
(*Spoken, seeing* FALSTAFF.) Off with your head!

FALSTAFF / AUSTIN
My head, my lord?

HENRY VIII / REED
Sorry, no. Force of habit. Be on your way. Storm be gone!
(*Ghostly; as he exits.*) Oooh – !

FALSTAFF / AUSTIN
The spirits have done it all in one night. I'm as giddy as a
drunken man. Who am I kidding? I am a drunken man! But
how do I escape these accursed woods?

                (POMPEY *enters.*)

POMPEY / TEDDY
Wow! That tempest was better than Splash Mountain. What
  a ride!

FALSTAFF / AUSTIN
Captain! Have you a ship nearby?

POMPEY / TEDDY
Ay, miraculously unharmed and anchored safely in the harbor.

FALSTAFF / AUSTIN
(*giving him* DROMIO'S *gold*) I'll pay for passage and new
  wardrobe besides.

POMPEY / TEDDY
Ay-ay! We'll sail on the outgoing tides!
(*Handing him hat and wig.*) What's your name now, since
  we're not looking back?

FALSTAFF / AUSTIN
(*putting on hat and wig*) Once I was Sir John, now – I'm
  Captain Jack!

(*He looks like a pirate. They exit.*)

SCENE 31: ACT FIVE, 2243: THE WOODS
(LADY MACBETH, HAMLET, 1ST WITCH, JULIUS CAESAR,
3RD WITCH, ARIEL, PUCK, PROSPERO, OBERON, 2ND WITCH,
SHAKESPEARE, MALVOLIAGO)

LADY MACBETH *enters, lost in the woods and crazed.*

LADY MACBETH / REED
These woods are like a nightmare, like a dream
In which I walk in slumb'ry agitation
And find no place to sit. Yet here's a spot.

(*A dog barks.*)

Out, damn'd Spot! Shoo, I say!

(HAMLET *enters, also lost.*)

LADY MACBETH / REED
My liege! Great Dane!

HAMLET / AUSTIN
        My lady! Still sane?

LADY MACBETH / REED
(*giving a 'more or less' gesture*) Eh . . .

(1ST WITCH *enters.*)

1ST WITCH / TEDDY
Lady Macbeth! Dear Puck said you'd be here.

HAMLET / AUSTIN
How now, you mad harpy? What brings you near?

1ST WITCH / TEDDY
A little of this, a little of that.

HAMLET / AUSTIN
Answer me! I need to know something – stat!
Will I become king?

LADY MACBETH / REED
             Will you make me glad?

1ST WITCH / TEDDY
Well, I've got some good news and some bad.
No man of woman born shall harm Hamlet.

(1ST WITCH *cackles and exits.*)

HAMLET / AUSTIN
No man of woman born? Well, that's everyone!

LADY MACBETH / REED
There's not a man who can harm you, not one!

HAMLET / AUSTIN
I wonder what the bad news is . . .

(JULIUS CAESAR *enters.*)

CAESAR / TEDDY
Cowards die many times before their deaths;
The valiant never taste of death but once.

HAMLET / AUSTIN
I'm not afeard, not of you nor your army!

(CAESAR *stabs* HAMLET, *who throws out red
ribbons to indicate the blood.*)

HAMLET / AUSTIN
Wait! The witch said that no man can harm me!

CAESAR / TEDDY
I was from mother's womb untimely ripp'd.
That's why Caesarean birth is named for me.

AUSTIN / REED
Oh!

HAMLET / AUSTIN
I bet that was the bad news.

LADY MACBETH / REED
Maybe.

(CAESAR *stabs* HAMLET *again, who throws
out more red ribbons and exits.*)

LADY MACBETH / REED
Who would have thought the young man to have had so
much blood in him?

CAESAR / TEDDY
You are my empress and a great beauty.

LADY MACBETH / REED
(*admiring his backside*) You've quite a backside –

CAESAR / TEDDY
                    Et tu your booty.

                    (*He slaps her on the arse. As they turn
                    upstage to exit . . .*)

LADY MACBETH / REED
Ooh, is this your dagger I see before me?

CAESAR / TEDDY
Hey-o!

                    (3RD WITCH *enters.*)

3rd WITCH / AUSTIN
(*singing*) Oh the witch, the witch, the witch is back!
Stone cold evil as a matter of fact – yeah!
(*When there's little reaction.*)
Come on, that kills at karaoke!

                    (ARIEL *enters.*)

Why, how now? Ariel! Why are you here?

ARIEL / TEDDY
Simply to tell you that all is forgiven.
Prospero's freed me and now I'll start livin'.

3RD WITCH / AUSTIN
You're very sweet. Here, take this mere token,
And no more of this will e'er be spoken.

                    (*She hands* ARIEL *the strawberry
                    handkerchief.*)

ARIEL / TEDDY
(*touched*) Why, thank you, hag. Our enmity is done.

3RD WITCH / AUSTIN
You've got ninety-nine problems but a witch ain't one!

> (*She cackles.* PUCK *enters, surprised to see
> them.*)

PUCK / REED
I didn't expect to find you together.
(*he sneezes; frustrated*)
I caught a cold from all that rough weather.

ARIEL / TEDDY
(*handing him the handkerchief*)
Here. Let our bitterness be forgotten.

3rd WITCH / AUSTIN
No! Wait – !

PUCK / REED
    Let us now stop acting rotten.

3RD WITCH / AUSTIN
But I want – I mean, *you* want revenge on Ariel!

PUCK / REED
Shh!!

ARIEL / TEDDY
    What?!

3rd WITCH / AUSTIN
    Oh, was I not supposed to tell?

ARIEL / TEDDY
(*to* PUCK) There's no way to trust the words that you spout.

3RD WITCH / AUSTIN
I'll just leave you two to sort this all out.

(3RD WITCH *cackles and exits.*)

ARIEL / TEDDY
I drop my guard, lies continue to grow.

PUCK / REED
I said that revenge thing a long time ago!
I'm nothing like that witch has portrayed me.

ARIEL / TEDDY
I can't believe it, you have betrayed me
Again! This final insult cannot stand.
I call forth all the magic I command!

(*She casts a spell. Chimes and thunder
sound. Lights probably flash too.*)

PUCK / REED
Careful! Don't let things get out of control!

ARIEL / TEDDY
You can't be trusted! You've an evil soul!

PUCK / REED
Pixie, take heed how you impawn our person,
How you awake our sleeping staff of war.

ARIEL / TEDDY
We charge *you* take heed for never two such
Kingdoms did contend without much fall of blood.

PUCK / REED
Master Oberon! I summon you now
To bring the rabble o'er whom you have power
Here to this place and incite them to motion!

(*He casts a spell too. More sound and lights.*)

ARIEL / TEDDY
(*also casting spells*) Mighty Prospero! Teach Puck a lesson!

PUCK / REED
Oberon's King of the Fairies, you know!

ARIEL / TEDDY
Yet no match for my master Prospero!
You will bow down before his sorcery!

PUCK / REED
Not if I call on the Weird Sisters three
To help Oberon put an end to thee!

(*As the noise and flashes reach their crescendo . . .*)

BOTH
Spirits! End this! Once and for all –
Show us the most powerful magician of all!

(*Thunder. The lights swirl and settle on a special down centre. Instead of* OBERON *or* PROSPERO, *the cloaked figure stands there. He removes his hood, revealing the politician's son turned glover's apprentice turned journeyman actor turned dramatic poet; the most powerful wizard-magician-genius-author-god in this or any universe –*

– WILLIAM SHAKESPEARE *himself.*

He wears the familiar ruff, hairpiece, and facial hair we associate with the known portraits of the Man from Stratford.)

PUCK / REED
Oh my Bard!

Ariel / Teddy
It is He!

Puck / Reed
That greatest Magician –

Ariel / Teddy
The only Begetter of us all –

Puck / Reed
The Man from Stratford himself –

Both
William Shakespeare!!
(*Dropping to their knees.*) We're not worthy, we're not
  worthy!

Shakespeare / Austin
(*re: the audience*) O wonder!
How many goodly creatures are there here!
How beauteous mankind is! O brave new world,
That has such people in't.
It's a world of laughter, a world of tears,
It's a world of hopes and a world of fears.

Ariel / Teddy
It is a small world after all! Master, I have done my spriting
  badly!

Puck / Reed
No, gracious king, 'tis I who have pucked up!

Shakespeare / Austin
Yes, confusion hath marred my masterpiece.
The fault, dear fairies, is not in your powers
But in ourself. You are my creations,
And your magic's as wild and uncontrolled
As my genius is. Yes, I'm young and bold,
But my skill's still naive and slightly daft.
My imagination o'erwhelms my craft.
Thus, I stand before you as a living

Post-modern and meta-theatrical
Coup d'theatre deus ex machina,
Who doth walk in and talk in a
Good earnest manner. Here is the matter:
I wrote myself into a corner, so
I wrote myself into the play to get
Myself out of it. Because now I see
You must not be confined by me
In one tragic-historical-comedy.
It is clear to me now that for a start
You in separate plays must be set apart.
(*He gets the manuscript.*)
Because such greatness lies in every scene,
Divide we our play in three times thirteen.
So from now on, until the end of time,
I'll people not one play but thirty-nine!
Or forty, or forty-one, forty-two:
Loves's Labors Won and *The Lion King*, too!

PUCK / REED
Tell me, what fate awaits the Duke of Gloucester?

SHAKESPEARE / AUSTIN
Ah, Richard. By all accounts he was nice,
But if I write him that way I'll die. Twice.
From now on the legend, not fact, will stick:
Richard the Third's not a Duke, he's a dick.
Likewise, Henry the Eighth's such a bother:
He's my sovereign Elizabeth's father.
I can't portray him abusing his power,
Not if I don't want to die in the Tower.
I'll make his play so terrible that then
No one will ever perform it again.

ARIEL / TEDDY
What shall betide the Prince of Denmark?

SHAKESPEARE / AUSTIN
Lord Hamlet, I think, shall get his own play.
I could watch him weigh his options all day.

(*Flipping through the manuscript.*)

And this tempest's too good to use just once.
Likewise cross-dressing and similar stunts
Like potions and shipwrecks and a lost twin:
That will be how half of my plays begin.
Some are born great, some achieve greatness,
And others have greatness thrust upon them.
But not Timon of Athens. He's terrible.
And King Lear's daughters will not be witches,
But they'll still act like total spoiled brats.
The Weird Sisters, with their crazy dark passions,
They'll be TV's *Keeping Up with Kardashians.*

PUCK / REED
Are we real, or part of some made-up tale?

SHAKESPEARE / AUSTIN
I did create you all, including Dale.

PUCK / ARIEL   Woah!

(*They make a 'mind-blown' gesture.*)

SHAKESPEARE / AUSTIN
As no magic's mightier than my pen,
Your tales will be told again and again
And thy legacy live, outlasting death.
You'll survive longer than all who draw breath.
The greatest gift I can bestow on thee:
You – in fact we *all* – shall immortal be.
But now, what to do with this massive tome?
I cannot bequeath it or take it home
And give to Anne with my second-best bed.
It must not be staged, or worst of all, read.
So this rough magic I here abjure. I'll
Bury it certain fathoms in the earth,
And deeper than did ever plummet sound
I'll drown my book in a hole in the ground.
That way, no one shall ever see my play.
At least, that is, until this very day.

(*With a regal wave,* SHAKESPEARE *exits.*)

ARIEL / TEDDY
Immortal Bard! He has set things aright,
All seems a dream on this midsummer night!

PUCK / REED
'Tis true, he's saved both Puck and Ariel!
(*Taking out the handkerchief and waving it.*) So let's finally
   say, all's well that ends well!

> (*BANG! A shot rings out.* MALVOLIAGO *has
> entered and shot* PUCK, *who falls to the
> floor. He exits as* ARIEL *goes to* PUCK.)

ARIEL / TEDDY
Malvoliago!

(*cradling the dying Puck – simply yet earnestly*)
               Oh, my gentle Puck,
Mischievous Puck! Sleep, my love? Dead, my dove?
I know when one is dead, and when one lives;
He is dead as earth. He's gone forever!
The breaking of so great a thing should
Make a greater crack. O, I would not wish
Any companion in the world but you.
Why should a dog, a horse, a rat, have life
And thou no breath at all? No, not in death,
The undiscovered country you shan't dwell
Without your rival, now friend, Ariel!
You've still life left, many years aplenty.
You want thingamabobs? I've got twenty!
They're all yours, gentle Puck. But you can't leave!
(*Leaning in to hear.*)
What's that? You say you won't – if they believe?
If they believe in fairies?

> (*He drops* PUCK *to the ground and leaps up.*)

ARIEL / TEDDY
               That will happen

If we can get the audience clappin'?
(*To the audience.*) Come, help me release him from his bands
With the help of your good hands!
Clap, don't let Puck die! Clap!

> (*The audience applauds.* PUCK *wakes and rises to one knee.*)

PUCK / REED
(*to* ARIEL) Give me your hand, for we be friends
And Robin shall restore amends.

> (*He leaps up. They embrace.*)

ARIEL / TEDDY
I do love nothing in the world so much as you. Is not that strange?

PUCK / REED
As strange as the thing I know not. I was about to protest I lov'd you!

ARIEL / TEDDY
And do it with all thy heart.

PUCK / REED
I do it with so much of my heart that none is left to protest –

ARIEL / TEDDY
Peace. Come on and kiss the girl.

> (*They kiss.* SHAKESPEARE *appears.*)

SHAKESPEARE / AUSTIN
Oi! Get thee a room!

> (*He disappears.* PUCK *mouths "hold that thought" to* ARIEL *and turns to the audience.*)

PUCK / REED
If we players have offended,
That's tough luck, you've all attended,
And some of you but slumber'd here,
Crinkled wrappers, scratched your rear,
So you missed the epic themes,
Romantic stories, evil schemes,
But we will not reprehend:
What's the point? This is the end:
And, as I am an honest Puck,
Then I say, oh, what the . . . hell,
For we 'scape the critic's tongue,
'Cuz Shakespeare's plays are ever young;
Else the Puck a liar call.
So, good night unto you all.
Now, to friends you can finally say,
"I saw Shakespeare's long lost first play."

> (*Music starts.* PUCK *and* ARIEL *start to bow,
> then almost have a moment of conflict
> before they warmly embrace, bow, then exit
> dancing.*
>
> SHAKESPEARE *enters, holding a quill pen. He
> bows, drops the quill like he's dropping the
> mic and exits as –*
>
> LEAR *hobbles on and starts frenetically
> break-dancing. He grabs his back, says,
> "I'm okay!" and exits as –*
>
> MISTRESS QUICKLY *dances on, followed by*
> FALSTAFF. *She twerks in front of him, and
> they exit as –*
>
> PETRUCHIO *dances on, doing the Robot. He
> says "Buh-bye!" and exits as –*
>
> DROMIO *dances on as* DROMIO OF EPHESUS
> *enters, dancing and dressed identically*

*as his brother. They see each other, yell
"Dromio!", embrace, and exit as –*

The 2ND WITCH *enters, followed by the* 3RD
AND 1ST WITCHES. *They dance downstage and
take a big bow. While they're down, they
take off their hoods and masks and puppets
and resume standing as* REED, AUSTIN, *and*
TEDDY.

They bow a final time, yell "Buh-bye!" like
PETRUCHIO, *and exit. End of show.*)